Love & Gifts

Love & Gifts

Jim McNair

BETHANY FELLOWSHIP, INC.
Minneapolis, Minnesota

Published by Bethany Fellowship, Inc.
6820 Auto Club Road, Minneapolis, Minnesota 55438

Printed in the United States of America

Library of Congress Cataloging in Publication Data:

McNair, Jim, 1934-
    Love and gifts.

    Includes bibliographical references.
    1. Gifts, Spiritual—Biblical teaching. 2. Love
(Theology)—Biblical teaching. I. Title.
BS2545.G47M3   234'.1   76-6555
ISBN 0-87123-328-2

We wish to acknowledge the use of the following copyrighted publications; quotations from them are identified by symbols in parentheses.

(RSV) THE HOLY BIBLE: REVISED STANDARD VERSION (New York, N.Y.: Thomas Nelson & Sons, 1952).

(NASB) NEW AMERICAN STANDARD BIBLE (Carol Stream, Ill.: Creation House, 1971).

(NEB) THE NEW ENGLISH BIBLE (New York, N.Y.: Oxford Univ. Press, 1961).

(TAB) THE AMPLIFIED BIBLE (Grand Rapids, Mich.: Zondervan, 1965).

(TEV) GOOD NEWS FOR MODERN MAN—THE NEW TESTAMENT IN TODAY'S ENGLISH VERSION (New York, N.Y.: American Bible Society, 1966).

Scripture quotations are from the Revised Standard Version unless otherwise indicated.

James Warwick McNair is a resident of New Zealand. He was ordained as a Baptist minister following two years of Bible college work and four years of theological seminary. He holds an L. Th. degree from the Melbourne College of Divinity.

Rev. McNair has served Baptist churches in two locations in New Zealand, and is currently involved in teaching, preaching, and counseling on an interdenominational level.

Preface

This book began some years ago as the result of a growing hunger for a deeper knowledge of God. The notes made then on the subject of the Holy Spirit and His ministry were later to provide the basis for this writing.

My own needs and the needs of fellow pastors and of churches everywhere had convinced me that we did not have, nor did we expect, the same dynamic that the early church had. The New Testament reveals that the Lord has made great provision for His people. Yet all around us many of God's people are living in exile "for want of knowledge; their honored men are dying of hunger, and their multitude is parched with thirst" (Isa. 5:13). Tens of thousands of them are grappling with the same questions, misunderstandings and prejudices on the Holy Spirit's ministry that we struggled with, and many are still searching for reality.

The Scriptures soon brought a deeper appreciation of the Spirit's work, which in turn resulted in my wife and me entering a completely new dimension of Christian experience where the Lord Jesus Christ became more real to us both. The Word of God that we loved before was even more satisfying than we had expected. And yet with the new dimension we became aware that we had hardly started! Much land remained—and, I might say, remains—to be possessed.

As long as the Church overlooks its rich resources in Christ through the power of the Spirit, it must accept some of the responsibility for the fact that it in turn is frequently overlooked as a source of reality. Yet all the while Jesus Christ remains the same today as He was yesterday! God has provided His church with spiritual weapons to defeat the enemy. His power remains undiminished, and all the craving for supernatural reality that He has built into our hearts can be met completely from His supply.

This book is presented to clarify some important aspects of biblical teaching on the Spirit's ministry, and to unfold something of His significance in the experience of the believer.

It is our prayer that these pages will nourish faith, feed minds, deepen experience of the Lord, and intensify the desire for the power of the Holy Spirit and the love and gifts He imparts, so that the Church can exercise these in humility, holiness and harmony for the glory of our Lord Jesus Christ.

I am deeply grateful for the friends who have made many helpful suggestions and checked earlier drafts of the manuscript. Above all, gratitude is expressed to my wife, Joy, for her love, help and example, and to our three children, Karen, Lynn and Peter, for their willingness to forego time with their dad.

The researching and writing of this book and its practical application in ministry to the Lord and others has been a joy. It has opened to me something of the inexhaustible greatness of God the Father, Son and Holy Spirit, and of the provision He lavishes upon us. May the reading of it do something of that for others.

Contents

1

Spiritual Gifts and Unity

1 CORINTHIANS 12

The Corinthian Christians lived amid a decadent society. Corinth was one of the most immoral cities of the ancient world, and the church had been drawn from this background.

"Do not be deceived," Paul wrote. "Neither the immoral, nor idolaters, nor adulterers, nor homosexuals, nor thieves, nor the greedy, nor drunkards, nor revilers, nor robbers will inherit the kingdom of God. And such were some of you" (6:9-11). °

These Christians were now called out to belong to a holy Lord and Savior, but the process of being freed from the degradation of their past associations was still continuing. Much still needed correction. They were making very real progress, but like some of the athletes at the famous games held in Corinth, they had started on handicap. Leon Morris reminds us that:

> Although much was still amiss in the lives of the Corinthian believers, there is no reason for doubting that the Christian community at Corinth must have presented, as a whole,

---

° Scripture references in the first three chapters are from 1 Corinthians unless otherwise indicated.

a marvellous contrast to their heathen fellow-citizens and
Paul gives sincere thanks for this.[1]

We must not think that Corinth was the only church which
found difficulty adjusting to a completely new way of life
and overcoming the problems inherited from earlier associations. For example, after his lengthy ministry among the
Ephesians, Paul reminded them of the continual burden he
had for them: "For three years I did not cease night or
day to admonish every one with tears" (Acts 20:31). If he
had detailed the particulars concerning which he personally
admonished them with tears, we could well possess a record
of their shortcomings similar to that of the Corinthians.
Paul in fact gave some painfully relevant instruction regarding their elementary shortcomings when he wrote to the
Ephesians. Clearly they were still being tempted to go back
to living futile, darkened lives like the Gentiles. They needed
further exhortations to discard the old nature with its deceitful lusts, and to abstain from sins such as evil talk, slander
and falsehood. It was still necessary to instruct them to
refrain from stealing, anger, bitterness, immorality, drunkenness, and grieving the Holy Spirit (Eph. 4:1-5:18). Later,
the ascended Lord reproached them for having abandoned
their first love (Rev. 2:1-7).

Other New Testament letters show that churches besides
those in Corinth and Ephesus also needed practical instruction and reminders of the necessity to be transformed by
yielding to God (e.g., Rom. 6:13; 12:2; Col. 3).

It is therefore misleading to disparage the Corinthian
church as less spiritual and more beset by problems than
others simply because Paul had to deal with its weaknesses
by correspondence. Believers in every age must, of course,
take seriously the Corinthians' faults and the divine pre-
scriptions for their cure, but no one can take a superior
attitude unless he has emerged from a similar society with
greater victory.

Paul himself had earlier gone to Corinth to preach Christ,

and for eighteen months[2] he had labored there. Then about A.D. 54/55, during his three-year ministry at Ephesus (16:8), he addressed this letter to the Corinthian church but expanded its application to "all those who in every place call on the name of our Lord Jesus Christ" (1:2). This means, of course, that Paul's message to the Corinthians was the same as he would give to the Ephesians and Colossians, just as the truths shared with the latter churches were equally for all other Christians (see 4:17).

Paul's Corinthian letter is both practical and timely. Like other portions of scripture, it is "inspired by God and profitable for teaching, for reproof, for correction, and for training in righteousness, that the man of God may be complete, equipped for every good work" (2 Tim. 3:16-17). It has much to teach us.

Concerning Spiritual Gifts in General (12:1-3)

1-3. Now concerning spiritual gifts, brethren, I do not want you to be uninformed. You know that when you were heathen, you were led astray to dumb idols, however you may have been moved. Therefore I want you to understand that no one speaking by the Spirit of God ever says "Jesus be cursed!" and no one can say "Jesus is Lord" except by the Holy Spirit.

The Corinthians had written to Paul raising various questions, and Paul refers to these in turn and deals specifically with them throughout the letter (7:1, 25; 8:1; 12:1; 16:1, 12). *Now concerning spiritual gifts*—literally, "Now concerning the spirituals." This was one of the subjects on which they had asked direction. The form of the Greek word *pneumatikōn* (spirituals) can be either neuter (spiritual gifts) or masculine (spiritual persons). But as a "spiritual person" in Paul's view was someone ruled by the Holy Spirit with powers of discernment and spiritual gifts (2:12-14; Rom. 8:9-14), there is no appreciable difference in meaning.

I do not want you to be uninformed. Paul devoted a large

portion of his ministry to teaching and encouraging Christians to be "filled with the knowledge of his will in all spiritual wisdom and understanding, to lead a life worthy of the Lord, fully pleasing to him, bearing fruit in every good work and increasing in the knowledge of God" (Col. 1:9-10; see Phil. 1:9-11). Once we become Christians, we should endeavor with God's help to become as fully informed as possible about every area of our faith, and to be always ready to give account to any inquirer for the hope that we have (see 1 Pet. 3:15). As God's people we should love biblical doctrine, for it brings insight into God's mind and helps us become conformed to His image.

To be disciples of Christ means that we are learners, people under His instruction (Matt. 11:29; John 8:31-32). Any believer who would serve the Lord acceptably is called upon to love Him with all his mind as well as with all his heart, soul and strength (Mark 12:30-33), and to supplement his faith with knowledge (2 Pet. 1:5-6).

The correct exercise of spiritual gifts is important and Paul wants to alert his readers to more of God's truth, for ignorance of any of His provisions is no virtue. Prejudice, indifference and even antagonism can easily develop when understanding is limited (see Hos. 4:6; Isa. 5:13). Doubts or confusion may sometimes arise, not because we are unspiritual, but solely because our knowledge of God's Word is too limited. It was to the Corinthians' credit that they wanted apostolic answers to their questions.

The presence of the unusual, mystical or supernatural in itself is no proof of the presence and activity of God's Spirit. Paul contrasts the Corinthians' heathen past with their present trust in a living Jesus: *you were heathen, you were led astray to dumb idols.* In similar vein he wrote to the Ephesians:

> You were dead through the trespasses and sins in which you once walked, following the course of this world, following the prince of the power of the air, the spirit that is now at

work in the sons of disobedience. Among these we all once lived . . . We were dead . . . , separated from Christ, alienated . . . , strangers to the covenants of promise, having no hope and without God in the world. But now in Christ Jesus you who once were far off have been brought near in the blood of Christ (Eph. 2:1-5, 12-13).

And again:

Once you were darkness, but now you are light in the Lord; walk as children of light (Eph. 5:8).

In themselves the idols were dumb, without the power of speech or inspiration. They were nothing (1 Cor. 8:4), but the demonic powers of darkness behind them were very real (Eph. 6:12-13; Isa. 44:18-20) and well able to capitalize on the weakness of those who gave themselves over to idolatry. Such demonic spirits would take over and violate the personality, bringing loss of self-control, blindly propelling their victims and driving them to irresponsible actions and speech.

But the Christian way was in complete and glorious contrast to this compulsion, for the Holy Spirit cooperated with the believer and encouraged, helped and spoke to him, while never violating his freedom of choice or will. The Holy Spirit inspired quietly from within; therefore there was no suggestion of coercion, nothing frenzied, forced or frantic, with no need for striving as if God was always just out of reach. He was with them. In them. His indwelling was a complete contrast to the pressure of the powers of darkness previously so familiar.

Why did Paul introduce his discussion of spiritual manifestations by the assurance that *no one speaking by the Spirit of God ever says "Jesus be cursed!"*? The tone is that of reassurance as though it were a reply to a troubled questioner who was afraid something might be said that was irreverent or even blasphemous, especially in speaking in tongues. It is probably Paul's reply to a specific question on this point sent by some of the Corinthians who wanted to be doubly sure.

No one inspired by God's Spirit is indifferent to the Lord Jesus Christ, for the Wind of the Spirit always moves him in one direction—toward Jesus himself. Many fear to emphasize the Spirit's ministry, lest Jesus lose His preeminence. But no one magnifies the Lord as the Holy Spirit does, for as Jesus said of Him, "He will bear witness to me" and "He shall glorify me" (John 15:26; 16:14). Nothing contrary to the glory of the Lord Jesus will come from the Spirit of Jesus. He will never dishonor Him, for there is no rivalry within the Godhead.

No one can say "Jesus is Lord" except by the Holy Spirit. The assertion *Kurios Iēsous* can best be brought out in translation: *Jesus! Lord!* It is not a statement of doctrine, true though it would be, but the glad expression of ownership and worship. Whoever says "Jesus is Lord!" is saying simultaneously, "Jesus, you are the Lord of my life. I accept your authority. I proclaim myself your servant. I want nothing more, nothing less, nothing apart from your will." This total commitment to Jesus Christ, with all that is involved in the word "Lord" (*Kurios*), is the foundation for what Paul goes on to say about spiritual gifts. The purpose of the gifts and ministry of the Spirit will always be to point to another—to Jesus who is Lord, and to build us up in Him.

Spiritual Gifts Described (12:4-11)

4-6. Now there are varieties of gifts, but the same Spirit; and there are varieties of service, but the same Lord; and there are varieties of working, but it is the same God who inspires them all in every one.

Now there are varieties of gifts. Behind this word "gifts" (*charismata*, a different word from that also translated "gifts" in verse 1) is the thought of "grace." Grace (*charis*) is one of the richest theological words in the Bible. It means the redemptive action of God in Christ, whether in the incarnation, the cross, the resurrection, or in Christ's present ministry to us through the Spirit, or His final return in glory and the consummation of all things in Him. Whatever aspect is being considered, this word "grace" always refers to God's saving mercy extended to totally undeserving men, inviting them now to enjoy the multi-faceted privileges of His favor. This grace is intensely practical, for it involves itself in our human predicament and expresses God's actions in reaching out to us. As a consequence, we can be redeemed, forgiven, transformed, and experience eternal life in Christ on the basis of faith (Eph. 2:8-9). Thus grace refers to every operation of God's favor and each divine enabling in the Christian's life.

Sometimes this word *charis* (grace) is used in the particular sense of the related word *charisma* (e.g., Rom. 12:3, 6; 15:15; Eph. 4:7). This latter word means "gift of grace, grace-gift, gratuity, free favor, endowment." Within the New Testament the same word *charisma* is used both of such gifts as eternal life (Rom. 6:23), the gift of continence (1 Cor. 7: 7), and the list of supernatural gifts in this chapter. Eternal life is as much a supernatural gift as tongues or prophecy or the ability to live a single life. In other words, the supernaturalness may be expressed in a great variety of ways. Thus there are "regular" gifts which form part of our inheritance of grace in Christ, as well as the "extraordinary" powers experienced by the Spirit's special inspiration and enabling.[3]

God gives His grace-gifts (*charismata,* the plural form of *charisma,* and related as we saw to *charis*) to those who belong to Jesus Christ. The gifts all come unmerited from *the same Spirit,* and because of this, there is no room for rivalry, discontent or superiority. They are gifts, not rewards for special merit or spiritual progress. The slightest thought of personal merit in the recipient, the faintest suggestion that the blessings can be purchased through any bargain made by the believer is completely foreign to the whole concept of *charisma:* it is God's gift, the outflow and over- flow of His grace. All are expressions of His graciousness, the provision of something we desperately need but can never deserve. They are given, not because of our worth but *to bring God's people nearer to His divine perfection.*

There is a rich variety of gifts, and there are *varieties of services* or ministries to which the Lord calls His children. These are to enable them to minister to needs both within and outside His church. There are also varieties in the *out- workings* of these gifts, for they have different effects. Great variety is observed not only because different people express different gifts, but because different combinations of various gifts may be manifested by the same person.

Behind all this variety there is the activity of the Triune God: *the same Spirit . . ., the same Lord* (Jesus) . . ., *the same God* (the Father) who inspires all the gifts in every one.

7. To each is given the manifestation of the Spirit for the common good.

God inspires this rich diversity of grace-gifts, ministries and outworkings, *for the common good,* that is, for the profit, well-being and growth of the Christian community (Eph. 4:12-16). Of God's anointed Servant Jesus, it had been fore- told: "Thus says God, the Lord, . . . I have given you as . . . a light to the nations, to open the eyes that are blind, to bring out the prisoners from the dungeon, from the prison those who sit in darkness" (Isa. 42:5-7).

The Father wanted everyone to profit from the ministry of Jesus. When empowered by the Holy Spirit we in turn are to walk where Jesus walked—in His steps (1 Pet. 2:21) —and continue the work He began (Acts 1:1).

Manifestation translates *phanerōsis*, a word that can also be rendered, "an outward evidencing, clear display, obviousness, exhibition." In each Christian there should be some particular expression that makes the Spirit "tangible" and His reality obvious. Any such manifestation expresses the indwelling Holy Spirit. The gifts themselves are therefore not unnecessary adornments but *essential operations,* without which God's church cannot fully express the Spirit nor function properly. Coming from a God of infinite wisdom and love, gifts will never be useless, meaningless or superfluous, and coming from the Holy Spirit they will be holy and consistent with the Spirit's character. They encourage holiness and Christlikeness. *To each is given:* No one is excluded from the necessity of revealing the character and power of the Holy Spirit in at least one of the nine gifts that follow—though this, we will see, is a minimum, for it is possible to manifest more than one (e.g. 14:13). All Christians are to be participants; not one is to be a mere spectator.

8-10. To one is given through the Spirit the utterance of wisdom, and to another the utterance of knowledge according to the same Spirit, to another faith by the same Spirit, to another gifts of healing by the one Spirit, to another the working of miracles, to another prophecy, to another the ability to distinguish between spirits, to another various kinds of tongues, to another the interpretation of tongues.

The early Christians expected God to invade their worship and service. They knew that He was transforming them by His presence and inspiration and giving gifts that were needed to minister to Him and to others. When they worshipped together or faced some special need, they expected the Holy Spirit to express himself for their enrichment.

Both "word" or "utterance" are valid translations of *logos*, but "word" is the better rendering for words of wisdom and of knowledge because these will not always need to be uttered. For example, God can give a *logos* for utterance, but also for "pondering in the heart" (Luke 2:17-19), as a means of supplying helpful information (Acts 9:10-17), or as a subject for intercession.

The Word of Wisdom

This is not wisdom gradually acquired, nor growth in understanding God's Word. It does not come by study or any effort of our own, or by human experience. It does not involve drawing upon a store of human wisdom (James 3:17; 1 Cor. 1:20-21), even one reinforced by divine grace (James 1:5). Instead it is a sudden, miraculous, unpremeditated revelation of wisdom which is specially appropriate and given for a specific situation, not as a continuing possession.

Scripture supplies us with many examples. Solomon prayed, " 'Give thy servant therefore an understanding mind to govern thy people, that I may discern between good and evil. . . .' And God said . . . 'Behold, I give you a wise and discerning mind' " (1 Kings 3:9-12).

When two women came to Solomon with two babies, one dead and one alive, each mother insisted that the living child was her own, but a word of wisdom quickly brought God's answer to the dilemma! (1 Kings 3:16-28).

Often Jesus uttered a word of wisdom that silenced His opponents, and they asked in astonishment, "Where did this man get this wisdom?" (Matt. 13:54; see Luke 13:17; 14:6; 20:24-26, 34-40).

Again and again it appeared that the persecutors of the early Christians were not able to overthrow their testimony and defense. This accorded with Jesus' promise to give wisdom "which none of your adversaries will be able to withstand or contradict" (Luke 21:15). (Yet while their persecutors could prove nothing against the believers, the prejudice and blind hate caused them to suffer for Christ and to be imprisoned, beaten and sometimes killed.)

The word of wisdom refers to the supernatural *application* of knowledge. It is a revelation from God, usually revealing how and when facts already known are to be used. As such it is often given in association with the word of knowledge.

The Word of Knowledge

This is a sudden revelation by the Holy Spirit of certain facts relating to specific situations which were not learned through normal thought processes. It comes by revelation, not education or observation. (It is not a knowledge of God's written Word, since that comes by disciplined study and meditation.) This gift comes to warn of difficulty or danger, to reveal helpful information as to the best way of meeting others' needs, and to give insight as to how to pray.

Various examples amply demonstrate that "there is a God in heaven who reveals mysteries" (Dan. 2:28).

In Samuel we see the operation of a word of knowledge concerning Saul's future, his thoughts and his asses (1 Sam. 9:17-20).

Nathan was given a word of knowledge regarding David's sin with Bathsheba—a word that must have come with devastating directness (2 Sam. 12:7-14). Such a word was also given to Elisha after Gehazi's deception (2 Kings 5:20-27).

Again, Elisha received various words of knowledge about the position of the ambushes the Syrian army was setting up. This saved Israel from battle and defeat, and confused the king of Syria. Though the prophet was nowhere near, God gave immediate revelation so that Elisha could tell the king of Israel the words that he spoke in his bedchamber (2 Kings 6:8-12).

"How do you know me?" asked a startled Nathaniel

of a Jesus who knew his nature and his innermost thoughts yet had never previously met him (John 1:47-50).

The woman of Samaria heard a word of knowledge concerning her past life with convincing detail: "You have had five husbands, and he whom you now have is not your husband." She then testified to others: "Come, see a man who told me all that I ever did" (see John 4:17-19, 29).

By a word of knowledge, Peter was shown the deception and hypocrisy within Ananias and Sapphira. God used this to bring needed self-examination and cleansing in the early church (Acts 5:1-11).

A different Ananias received in a vision a word of knowledge giving Saul's name, the knowledge of his conversion, the name of the street where he was staying (Straight), the name of the man in whose home he could be located (Judas), what his physical condition was (he had lost his sight), what his spiritual condition was (repentant, prepared, waiting, prayerful), and his need (for healing and filling with the Holy Spirit) (Acts 9:10-17).

Through a word of knowledge, Peter learned that three men were looking for him and that he should accompany them immediately, for the Spirit himself had sent them (Acts 10:19-20).

Paul perceived by a word of knowledge that the hand of God's judgment was upon Elymas the magician who was openly opposing the gospel. It was revealed that he would become blind and unable to see the sun for a time (Acts 13:11). Paul knew that a needy cripple had "faith to be made well" and could be healed (Acts 14:8-9). On another occasion he knew that though the ship they were traveling in would be lost, neither passengers nor crew would lose their lives (Acts 27:22-44).

Though words of knowledge and of wisdom frequently operate together and complement one another, they are quite different. This difference is illustrated in the well-known story of Solomon's dealing with the two insistent women who claimed the same child. In suggesting cutting the child in two to give each woman half, he was giving a word of wisdom. If he had received a word of knowledge, he would have been able to say directly, "That child belongs to that woman" (see 1 Kings 3:16-28).

The Gift of Faith

Faith is the characteristic of all Christians, for they are *believers* saved by faith (Rom. 3:22; 6:23). The gift of faith, however, is something more: it is an instantaneous and outstanding impartation from God, given on occasions to enable a Christian to believe God in a special way for the accomplishment of some specific task. By it, that which is visualized in the Spirit becomes a tangible reality which can be seen, heard, touched. What is known to faith has become fact, and can be appropriated. It is mountain-moving faith.

It is the faith that enabled Elijah to announce to Ahab, "There shall be neither dew nor rain these years, except by my word" (1 Kings 17:1; see James 5:17). Again, this faith was given when he drenched the sacrifice in the contest against the prophets of Baal upon Mount Carmel (1 Kings 18:27-35).

Further gifts of faith were manifested by Noah, Abraham, Moses, Rahab, Gideon, Barak, Samson, David, Samuel and the prophets (see Heb. 11).

The gift was seen in countless ways throughout the earthly life and ministry of Jesus—for example, in the raising of a rapidly decomposing Lazarus (John 11:41-44) and the destiny of a fig tree that withered when He spoke (Matt. 21:18-21).

Other examples in the Gospels and in the life of the early church abound (see Matt. 17:27; Acts 3:6-7; 9:40).

Often this gift is closely linked with working of miracles.

Gifts of Healings

Through this gift God instantaneously heals people of their sickness. It is not to be confused with praying for and anointing the sick, when healing may not be immediate.

Jesus demonstrated love and compassion as He "went about doing good and healing all that were oppressed by the devil" (Acts 10:38). And He sent forth His disciples to do the same (Matt. 10:1, 7-8), for He loved the sick man's body as well as his soul.

To spread the important ministry of healing, God gives *gifts* of *healings*. (Both words are in a plural form.) One who is gifted in the healing ministry is rarely used in every area of healing, for there are different kinds of restoration. One may have a ministry in areas such as mental and emotional sickness, another among the crippled, another in the healing of internal ailments. Each healing is a fresh gift from the Lord.

Physical healings were used by the Lord in many different ways for a variety of purposes. Gifts of healings demonstrated the love of God in Christ, showed that God involved himself in all that concerns His children, comforted those in terrible distress (Matt. 8:3, 6-7), destroyed part of the devil's work in a human body (Acts 10:38), verified Jesus' verbal claims (John 10:37-38), complemented the spoken word (Acts 4:29-30), testified to Jesus' resurrection and His continuing presence and power (Acts 3:15-16), attracted people to hear the gospel (John 6:2; Acts 3:9-10), and were instrumental in turning people to the Lord (Acts 9:34-35) and bringing glory to God (Mark 2:12; Luke 13:17; Acts 4:21-22).

The Working of Miracles

This refers to the working of special powers granted by the Lord so that dynamic acts are performed in His name. Many examples could be given: the deliverance of Israel and the destruction of the Egyptians by the movement of the Red Sea waters (Ex. 14:21-31), the supply of water from the rock (Ex. 17:6), the crossing of the Jordan on dry ground (Josh. 3:15-4:18), the destruction of Jericho (Josh. 6:20-21), the sun and moon standing still at Joshua's command (Josh. 10:12-14), the widow's supply of oil and meal lasting throughout the time of famine (1 Kings 17:8-16), the sun returning ten degrees on Hezekiah's sundial (2 Kings 20:8-11).

Within the Gospels are the familiar miracles of turning water into wine, walking on the water, feeding the crowds of 5000 and 4000, calming the storm, finding money in the fish's mouth, and the miraculous catch of fish. There are many other signs both listed and unspecified (see John 20:30-31).

Many miracles also took place among the early Christians (e.g., Acts 2:43; 8:39-40). In fact the Church made the performance of signs and wonders a matter for prayer, requesting the moving of God's hand that signs and wonders might be performed through the name of God's holy servant Jesus (Acts 4:30-33).

Prophecy

Prophecy enables a believer to convey God's message to men in their own native language. It is a supernatural, unpremeditated endowment to tell forth that which does not originate in the speaker's mind. The message may concern the future (in which case we could term it *predictive prophecy*), but more commonly it applies to the present.

The words themselves aid our understanding of the nature of the gift. The associated word *"prophet"* (from *pro*—before, in front of; *phēmi*—to speak) means "one who speaks before" (in the sense of place, not time); "one who stands in front of God as His mouthpiece and passes on God's message." He is God's spokesman. Similarly, prophecy is the *message* given by someone who stands in front of God as His mouthpiece.

The word "prophecy" is used in both a narrow and a broad sense. In the narrow sense, *prophecy is used of one gift only as distinct from other revelatory gifts.* There are clear examples of this: (1) In the present context of 12:8-10, prophecy is listed separately. (2) In 14:6 it is again distinguished from the broader term "revelation"—even though Paul later shows that it, too, comes by revelation. (3) In 14:3 prophecy is more naturally understood in its restricted sense, when it brings edification, encouragement and consolation.

In the broadest sense, *prophecy is used as a synonym for revelation or revelatory gifts in general,* covering *all* divinely inspired revelation and utterance. As such, it can, for example, include words of wisdom and of knowledge, prophecy in its narrow sense, and discerning of spirits.

In support of different revelatory gifts being included under the general term "prophecy," we note the following: (1) After the revelatory gift of a word of knowledge in which Jesus said, "You have had five husbands, and he whom you now have is not your husband," the woman of Samaria termed Jesus *a prophet* (John 4:17-19). (2) After the mockers blindfolded Jesus, they called upon Him to *prophesy* as to who struck Him. Here, prophecy refers to the revelatory gift of a word of knowledge (Matt. 26:67-68; Mark 14:65). (3) In what is termed prophecy, an unbeliever hears "the secrets of his heart" disclosed (1 Cor. 14:25). Prophecy at this point describes more precisely a word of knowledge revealed with such precision that the one to whom it is directed has no doubt that God knows his innermost secrets. Its purpose here is not confined to ministering edification, encouragement and consolation to believers. (4) Prophecy is also used of revelation in general in Paul's other epistles (e.g., 1 Tim. 1:18; 4:14; see also 2 Tim. 1:6-7; 1 Thess. 5:20).

Whether prophecy is narrowly or broadly defined, it consistently involves revelation from God, as the human channel utters words or thoughts directly inspired by Him.

The Ability to Distinguish Between Spirits

This gift is also translated "discernment of spirits," and it is frequently referred to by that name.

All believers must test the spirits and accept the right and reject the wrong (1 John 4:1; 1 Thess. 5:21). The Lord expects us to grow in understanding and insight so that we accept only what is consistent with Scripture and bears the inner witness of the Spirit. In Hebrews we read of the need for all to have this discernment:

> For though by this time you ought to be teachers, you need some one to teach you again the first principles of God's word. You need milk, not solid food; for every one who lives on milk is unskilled in the word of righteousness, for he is a child. But solid food is for the mature, for those who have their faculties trained by practice to distinguish good from evil (Heb. 5:12-14).

The ability to distinguish good from evil goes together with Christian maturity, and is a strong defense against false teaching.

But beyond this discernment, there is a special divine gift of discerning of *spirits*. Such a gift is immensely valuable, for when God is moving in sovereign and gracious power, Satan will be ever on the alert to insinuate himself into the work to bring confusion and counterfeit. He will try to come as an angel of light and blur the edges of our discernment. Therefore there is a real need for us to be equipped by the Holy Spirit so that we can know absolutely whether an utterance or an influence comes from a divine, human, or demonic source.

When this gift operates, the Church can know immediately whether a person is speaking under the Holy Spirit's inspiration, from "visions of their own minds" (Jer. 23:16), or even from a demonic influence (Acts 16:16-18). Even if revelations and signs and wonders are present, are they of God or of Satan? (See 2 Thess. 2:9; Rev. 16:14.) Is the preaching or teaching Spirit-prompted? For even a beloved disciple may sometimes speak with a mixture of that which is of God and that which the enemy has inspired (Matt. 16:16-23). The teaching itself may be correct but given in a wrong spirit. When this happens, the inspiration of the message is robbed of edifying power. The cause of this deficiency can be related to a problem of the flesh, satanic influence, or both. The gift of discernment of spirits will reveal in which area the problem really lies, and help in weighing what is said.

Besides this function of evaluation, this gift forms the basis of the deliverance ministry. Many evil spirits (also called "demons") were discerned by Jesus and then expelled. Jesus came to proclaim release to the captives and to set at liberty those who are oppressed by the enemy (Luke 4:18; Isa. 61:1). Discernment and deliverance from these spirits (described as evil, unclean, deaf and dumb spirits, spirits of infirmity, and such like) occupied a major place in His ministry. Many times those who were demonized in these ways experienced deliverance from that which imprisoned them. Within the early church the gift of discerning of spirits operated frequently. For example, Simon's wickedness was exposed instantly (Acts 8:20-23). Elymas was recognized as a son of the devil and an enemy of all righteousness, full of all deceit and villainy (Acts 13:10). Behind the perfectly true words of a girl was the influence of a spirit of divination that Paul recognized and then cast out (Acts 16: 16-18).

When God purposes it, the gift of discerning of spirits can give an immediate awareness of demonic influence. Someone may speak only a few ordinary words of greeting over the telephone and we may instantly know their problem is demonic and which spirit is operating. Or discernment may come regarding someone present at a meeting who is involved in immorality or in some occult practice, whose presence is causing a spiritual chill and affecting the group as a whole. The gift enables recognition of who it is and the basic cause of their oppression. The opportunity can then be given for personal ministry in the problem area. If the person does not want this, further revelation will indicate the most effective means of dealing with the situation.

Those who receive this gift should receive the same love and respect when they minister this way as when they minister in other ways, for their ministry is essential for the health of the Body. However, for their part, they have a great responsibility to exercise their gift with the gentleness, love and strength of Christ.

Speaking in Various Kinds of Tongues

Through the exercise of this gift there is the speaking forth from the human spirit in another language of that which the Holy Spirit himself has inspired and enabled.

"Speaking in tongues" and "the gift of tongues" are equivalent expressions. For example, the tongues listed here among the spiritual gifts are later referred to as "*speaking in tongues.*" "Speaking in tongues" is a term used for both private and public utterance, whether with or without interpretation (see 14:5, 13, 27-28; Acts 2:4; 10:46; 19:6).

Interpretation of Tongues

This is a complementary gift to speaking in tongues, and is required after the public utterance of tongues. Through interpretation, God gives to someone present the ability to communicate to the congregation the content of the tongues utterance.

These last two gifts refer not to a natural linguistic proficiency, but to a supernaturally given ability to speak or to interpret. Because Paul gives detailed teaching on both in 1 Corinthians 14, we will consider them further within that context.

A helpful arrangement of these nine gifts is as follows:

A. *Divine gifts that impart supernatural power to KNOW:*
   Word of wisdom
   Word of knowledge
   Ability to distinguish between spirits
B. *Divine gifts that impart supernatural power to ACT:*
   The gift of faith

  Working of miracles
  Gifts of healings
C. *Divine gifts that impart supernatural power to SPEAK:*
  Prophecy
  Various kinds of tongues
  Interpretation of tongues

Paul's purpose is not to imply that the gifts listed in these verses are superior or inferior to any other catalog of God-given gifts. Neither is he stating here the obvious truth that all Christians have *natural* talents of differing kinds apart from those mentioned in these verses, nor that these are the *only* gifts the Spirit gives, but he regards it as basic that each could manifest at least one of *these* nine specific gifts. These spiritual gifts are not natural talents: they are supernatural and their operation requires divine initiative and enabling.

From what we know of Paul's life, it seems he exercised all or almost all of these gifts. Only interpretation of tongues is missing in the record of his ministry, and this omission is probably of no significance.

11. All these are inspired by one and the same Spirit, who apportions to each one individually as he wills.

The Spirit distributes these gifts where, when and as *He* wants to, not necessarily as *we* want (see 12:18, 28; Heb. 2:4). The distribution is in the hands of the Spirit of wisdom who best knows what is needed. In one meeting a particular Christian may prophesy, while on the next occasion the Lord may give him interpretation, or he may receive the ability to distinguish between spirits. Because someone expresses say, a word of knowledge this time, it does not mean God will minister the same gift through him the next time: He may, but He may not, for it is the Spirit who apportions to each one individually as He wills. On the other hand it may well be that a believer ministers mainly within the area of one particular gift. It has been well said that we do not *possess* the gifts: the gifts are for the people who need the edification, healing, and so on. We are simply "God's delivery men" who deliver the manifestation to meet the need God sees.

Unity in the Midst of Diversity of Gifts (12:12-31).

The unity of the Church is a unity in the midst of diversity, as the analogy of the human body illustrates. Within the body this unity and diversity quite naturally go together.

12. For just as the body is one and has many members, and all the members of the body, though many, are one body, so it is with Christ.

To make known the love of God on earth in concrete ways, Jesus took upon himself a perfect human body (see Phil. 2:7). Through the ministry of that body God was glorified upon the earth as Jesus showed the world what God was like (John 17:4). God was loving, good and powerful, and these attributes were expressed through His human body. But in order to show *continuing* generations the same love, goodness and power, Jesus has a Body that consists of living human beings—"the church which is his body" (Eph. 1:22-23; 1 Cor. 12:27). God desires to see Jesus Christ in all His wholeness, character, authority and power manifested and magnified in His present-day Body. He purposes that *the Church* should so identify itself with its Head that it too can repeat:

> The Spirit of the Lord is upon *me*, because he has anointed *me* to preach good news to the poor. He has sent *me* to proclaim release to the captives and recovering of sight to the blind, to set at liberty those who are oppressed, to proclaim the acceptable year of the Lord (Luke 4:18-19).

Through the physical body of Jesus a diversity of gifts was expressed: Through the Body of Christ today this same diversity has power to transform a dead orderliness into a living organism which pulsates with life—the very life of Jesus, made possible by the Spirit.

Paul saw the ordered operation of the gifts, not as a cause of disunity, but as *necessary for the expression of the true unity and health of the Body of Christ* (see 12:7; 14:12).

13. For by one Spirit we were all baptized into one body—Jews or Greeks, slaves or free—and all were made to drink of one Spirit. (author's translation).

To be "baptized in (*en*) the Spirit" is one of the picturesque terms the Holy Spirit inspired to express what did in fact take place in the lives of believers: they experienced a real immersion, an inflooding, an invasion with the Spirit in a conscious and profound encounter with the Lord (see Matt. 3:11; Mark 1:8; Luke 3:16; Acts 1:5; 11:16, and here in verse 13). This was a vital and continuing ministry of Jesus (John 1:33; see 7:37-39).

Paul could be certain that *all* his readers had been baptized in the Holy Spirit since His flooding into the lives of the early Christians was always attended by obvious supernatural evidence. If they did not receive the Spirit in this way, immediate steps were taken to rectify the deficiency and bring them into the fullness of Christian experience (see Acts 8:14-18; 19:5-7).

In this verse Paul ponders the incredible truth that people from vastly different backgrounds, religious cultures and social status had each experienced the same Spirit and had been brought into one Body. Now they were to express their oneness and interrelationship through the varied manifestations of the one Spirit on whom they were dependent.

14. For the body does not consist of one member but of many.

Both in the human body and in the Body of Christ there

are unique functions that no other members can fulfill. All are interdependent, and rely on each other for their existence and survival.

15-20. If the foot should say, "Because I am not a hand, I do not belong to the body," that would not make it any less a part of the body. And if the ear should say, "Because I am not an eye, I do not belong to the body," that would not make it any less a part of the body. If the whole body were an eye, where would be the hearing? If the whole body were an ear, where would be the sense of smell? But as it is, God arranged the organs in the body, each one of them, as he chose. If all were a single organ, where would the body be? As it is, there are many parts, yet one body.

Dissatisfaction or feelings of inferiority about our gift of being a humble "foot" or "ear" is unwarranted, for we still have our particular function in and for the health of the Body. The human body would be weakened if even one organ were missing. On the other hand, the "body" would be horribly grotesque if it consisted of only one organ—for example, eyes, with no organs for hearing, smelling, eating, walking. Indeed, it would not be a body at all. Therefore, the variety of functions among members of the Body is essential and ought to be a source of joy to all. We should rejoice at the gifts of others (see v. 26) and pray that *every* expression of the Spirit's life will be present in our congregations (see 1:5-7).

The most important thing is that the Body is healthy and growing in the image of Christ. To discredit or disregard our own contribution is one way of questioning God's wisdom, for it is *God* who arranges and gives. It is one thing to desire further gifts (for example, prophecy), while using those already entrusted to us, but it is quite another to neglect or complain about those we can already exercise. It is God's will that there be variety, but He is sovereign and designs the distribution and working of that variety.

> **21-26.** **The eye cannot say to the hand, "I have no need of you," nor again the head to the feet, "I have no need of you." On the contrary, the parts of the body which seem to be weaker are indispensable, and those parts of the body which we think less honorable we invest with the greater honor, and our unpresentable parts are treated with greater modesty, which our more presentable parts do not require. But God has so adjusted the body, giving the greater honor to the inferior part, that there may be no discord in the body, but that the members may have the same care for one another. If one member suffers, all suffer together; if one member is honored, all rejoice together.**

In contrast to those who are dissatisfied with their gifts, those who seem to possess higher gifts and see themselves as an important "eye" or "head" must not look down on others with different gifts. They should have a common concern for one another, for the head could not be held high without the spine's support, and the eye would not be of much practical use unless it could guide the hands. Each is dependent on the others, so even if someone had greatly helped another through a notable gift, he should recognize that the grace-gift was from God. No member should think of himself as in any way superior. The self-satisfied must remember that God has given "special honour to the *humbler* parts" (v. 24, NEB). So in the church any seemingly less presentable members are to be specially respected and honored, even though theirs is sometimes a less spectacular or coveted ministry.

The gifts, like limbs of the body, are functional in character. When we walk, the legs are more important than the arms, and when we talk, the mouth is more important than the eyes. When we hear, the ears have greater value than the mouth. Likewise, *all* the spiritual gifts are needed—not just those which seem to us to be most desirable. Since all gifts are for the one Body, all members should exercise their ministry harmoniously. In short, the church would be unhealthy and unbalanced if it was obliged to make do with very limited gifts, and therefore a very limited ministry.

If a member suffers, the whole Body should feel the hurt and uphold that one with constructive love. If a member is honored, the Body should rejoice together over the honor granted to him. Even if we have not been honored in the same way, we are to rejoice that others have been, and pray that God will use them greatly.

It is equally important that those who exercise certain gifts do not despise or segregate those who do not. Such Christians need loving encouragement, teaching and ministry which will enable them to release their own gifts. If manifestations are missing or withheld, the whole church is deficient and weakened in some areas of spiritual life.

There needs to be the loving encouragement of those who are fearful and who feel they are even less than one-talent men; and sometimes there is need for loving disciplining and pruning of those who have more gifts, and whose God-confidence begins to lapse into unattractive self-confidence or worse. God wants everyone to be knit together as interrelated members of the Body so that the "many talents" man acknowledges his need of others, and genuinely rejoices to receive personal ministry and enrichment through some gift or teaching manifested by a "one talent" member (Col. 2:2, 19).

27. Now you are the body of Christ and individually members of it.

Fellowshipping Christians are not simply a group of people meeting together, neither are they "the body of Christians": they are *the Body of Christ—the Body through which*

He is visible, and which expresses in love and power that which He himself accomplished. Each Christian belongs to the Body: individually they are members of it. None of them can represent the whole, but together they make up the Lord's Body. Equally, none of them is excluded from their honored place.

Jesus is earlier pictured as the "head of every *man*" (11:3), but neither in 1 Corinthians nor in Romans is the thought developed that He is the Head of the *Body*. Within both these letters the human body analogy is used to illustrate the corporate life of Christians as the Body of Christ, and their dependence upon one another (Rom. 12:4-5). Yet in later letters such as Colossians and Ephesians the same analogy is used in another way to emphasize the relationship which the Church as the Body bears to *Christ* as the Head. Now He is the Head of the Body, the Church (see Col. 1:18; 2:19; Eph. 1:22; 4:15; 5:23). In both these differing ways the analogy is pressed into use—first in this way, then in another. Over all, Jesus is the supreme Head, active in superintending, controlling, co-ordinating, motivating and strengthening His Body by His Spirit, and causing His living members to react with increasing sensitivity and receptivity to His promptings.

28. And God has appointed in the church first apostles, second prophets, third teachers, then workers of miracles, then healers, helpers, administrators, speakers in various kinds of tongues.

It is not certain here whether Paul is speaking of the local or universal church, as he uses the word in both senses, but it is probable that its meaning alters as the text proceeds, referring to apostles in the universal church, and prophets in the local church. Reference to "first . . . , second . . . , third . . ." may refer to their order of importance or to the chronological order in which God appointed to the Church these first ministries: first, apostles; second, New

Testament prophets; and third, teachers. Probably both importance and chronological order are combined in Paul's thought. C. K. Barrett comments:

> The numerical sequence is pursued no further, possibly because, though Paul can place all the remaining gifts on a lower level than apostleship, prophecy and teaching, he does not feel that he must, or wishes to, distinguish narrowly between the lower gifts.[5] [For apostles, prophets and teachers, see the comments on Eph. 4:8-13 in chapter five of this book.]

Helpers probably refers to deacons within the church. *Administrators:* the Greek means "steering" and is used of steering or piloting a ship; hence those who govern the church. Probably this word refers to the one ministry known variously as overseers (bishops), elders or pastors—the variety of term depending upon what aspect of their ministry was being emphasized.[6] Helpers and administrators are best understood as representing deacons and pastors/elders, respectively, for otherwise they are not referred to at all, which would be highly unlikely.

At this point, Paul is mentioning not the charismatic *gifts of power* which the Lord gives to each Spirit-filled Christian, but *the people themselves* whom God appoints in the church (Eph. 4:11-14). God calls or appoints a person to a particular office (apostle, prophet, teacher) or service (workers of miracles, etc.); but to function in that office or ministry for the profit of all, each Christian must exercise the manifestations of the Spirit in addition to his own natural ability. For example, with the apostle are associated the gifts of power: the elder/pastor needs the gifts for overseeing, counseling, healing and feeding the flock; and the evangelist ministers in signs, healing and deliverance (Acts 8:4-8; 21:8)—the latter associated with discernment of spirits. Verses 8-10 refer to *our divine equipment* and verses 27-28 to *our divine appointment, calling or function* in the Body.

The *various kinds of tongues* are various genuine God-given languages that communicate thoughts and feelings in what may be either a language of men or of angels. Donald Gee writes:

> These gifts do not represent the wisdom of man in most conveniently meeting the needs he is personally conscious of; but they represent the wisdom of God in Christ providing for our deepest need from the standpoint of the throne. The inspired illustration is the human body (12:14-28). It is common knowledge that we need varied diet for perfect physical health and strength, and exercise of every faculty is needed for all-round development. Few attain this in the natural; the brain is highly developed at the expense of the body, or vice versa. *Some* mental or *some* physical powers are perfected and hardened by continual use, while others remain dormant and flabby. In the realm of things seen and temporal this may be immaterial; but in the realm of the unseen and eternal the consequences are much more grave. The Church needs all-round spiritual growth and activity to arrive at her destined perfection in Christ.[7]

In verse 28 and all of chapter 12, Paul is not dealing with what God has given solely to the Corinthians, but to *the Church in totality* and each local expression of it (e.g., 1:2; 1 Thess. 5:19-20; Rom. 1:11; 12:3-8; Heb. 2:4; 1 Pet. 4:10-11).

29-30. Are all apostles? Are all prophets? Are all teachers? Do all work miracles? Do all possess gifts of healing? Do all speak with tongues? Do all interpret?

Not all are apostles, prophets, teachers, or have special ministries. (The Greek shows the answer "No" is expected.) Here, the reference is—at least in the first three—to more official positions. Paul is not referring to those, for example, who prophesy, but to prophets. A man may prophesy without being recognized as a prophet, or teach sometimes without being recognized as a teacher, or receive an anointing to heal, yet not be considered as one with a more permanent healing ministry. Not all have the same office in the church. Neither do all exercise identical service within it.

In these verses the Lord is emphasizing that for the balanced working of the Body various gifts are distributed
among believers. Each has a particular manifestation to
bring. No individual or even a few have all the inspiration.

At times Paul refers to the use of tongues in private
worship. At other times he considers the gift operating for
the benefit of others in the church. Here in this chapter
the theme is *the edifying of the Body,* and the interrelationship of all members is for this purpose. No single member
or method is to monopolize the building up of the Body.
In verse 28 he says, "God has appointed in the church . . .
prophets"—and now follows the question, "Are all prophets?" No!, not all have the ministry of a prophet, but all
may prophesy. Similarly, "Do all speak in tongues?"—that
is, do they *all* exercise the gift in authoritative public utterance in the church? Again, the answer is No—though as
we will see later, when the gift is confined to the realm
of an individual's communication with God, it is clear that
all may do so.

Scripture never suggests that a person is limited to only
one gift, but Paul guards against any speculation that some
may eventually be able to exercise all the necessary manifestations. They should remember that the church is a Body,
and that no one person will ever monopolize the ministry
and inspiration necessary for its health and growth.

God had deliberately designed the Body to be interdependent, with each member and his ministry needing each
of the others for balance and completion. Even if one could
prophesy, for example, it would not mean that all prophecy
must come through him. Others would also be used this
way, for no one person can manifest the whole Christ.

**31. But earnestly desire the higher gifts. And I will
show you a still more excellent way.**

The command is given to *earnestly desire the higher
gifts* (plural). This demonstrates that there is more than
the simple gift of prophecy in the higher gift category. It

is probable that Paul is here regarding the greatest gifts as the gifts most needed at the particular time. When the human body needs to see, the best gift is eyes; when we need to speak, the best gift is the mouth. Sometimes the ability to distinguish between spirits will be the pressing need and the gift a greater gift than prophecy in its narrower sense. Other times prophecy, a word of wisdom or of knowledge or some other gift may meet the most pressing need, or bring the greatest glory to the Lord. After tongues in public utterance, the greatest and most important gift to be desired and prayed for is interpretation of tongues (see 14:13, 5). *Earnestly desire:* The word *zēloō* here and in 14:1 means "to desire earnestly, strive for, be ambitious to acquire, be zealous for." It stresses the intensity of the action.

Paul is saying, "Earnestly desire the higher gifts and I will show you a more excellent way of manifesting gifts than the poorer way you Corinthians have been following up until now. Because of your self-interest and desire to be conspicuous and superior, you have been blind to the needs of others. I'm going to show you a more adequate motive for earnestly desiring, obtaining and using the gifts—the better way of love, which gives itself for others and adds depth and power to gifts and ministries."

It is sometimes said that love is the greatest of the gifts and therefore if we have love, other gifts become more or less optional or incidental. But this is a misunderstanding and creates confusion, for love itself is never described as a gift of the Spirit. Neither is it ever described as being a more important gift than prophecy or tongues, for example. Love is part of the *harvest* or *fruit of the Spirit,* not a gift.

When God loved, it did not make His giving less important: instead, the gift of His Son is *the evidence* of His love (John 3:16), as is the gift of eternal life (Rom. 6:23). Paul clearly sets love above all the gifts, not as an alternative, but as a controlling principle and dynamic by which they are made effectual.

A doctor looks upon a patient and with heartfelt compassion longs to provide some medication to bring healing and relief to the sufferer, but there is none. He does not rationalize that the remedy is of no consequence as long as he has compassion. It is his compassion which makes him desire the best remedy there is. Then if a remedy is produced he will do all in his power to acquire it and apply it to the specific area of need.

Larry Christenson illustrates this well:

> Suppose a man is dying of thirst in the desert, and you are sent out to rescue him. Out you go, your heart overflowing with love and concern. You find the man. His tongue and lips are swollen. "Water! Water!" he gasps frantically. But you just go up and throw your arms around him and say, "Oh, we don't believe in the gifts, brother. We just want to *love you*." The gifts . . . are the very means which the Spirit has given us to express Christ's love in an effective and concrete way. Desiring the spiritual gifts is not a sign of spiritual immaturity, acceptable only in someone who has not yet learned the more excellent way of love. Rather, desire for the spiritual gifts is a sign that one *does* love—but knows that in himself he has nothing to give. He is like the "friend at midnight" (Luke 11:5ff.). He goes to God and says, "This friend of mine has come, and I have nothing to give him. I pray You, supply me with what he needs, that I may give it to him." He doesn't sit in his rocker piously saying, "If the Lord wants to give me any gifts, He will do it." No, he *goes*. He *asks*—until he receives. He *seeks*—until he finds. He *knocks*—until the door is opened. This is the wedding of love and desire which the apostle urges upon us in these chapters of First Corinthians.[8]

2

Love—The Essential Ingredient
1 CORINTHIANS 13

The "Love Chapter" is one of the most important chapters in the Bible. Unfortunately it is often removed from its context of spiritual gifts, and its powerful truths are considered in isolation. We can still learn much from such a study, but we should recognize that uppermost in Paul's thinking was the need for Christlike love as the motive behind every gift.

Sadly, the presence and operation of natural or supernatural gifts does not automatically mean that love is prompting their use. There may be many gifts, yet little love. Similarly, though it is too self-evident for Paul to state, it is just as possible for a fellowship that lacks spiritual gifts to be hard and loveless. Neither the presence nor absence of gifts can be used as an indication of love. When Paul wrote, he desired that there be no controversy, but that love and gifts flow in harmony.

Paul's Christian readers were immature and had vast needs. But not for a moment did he despair or dismiss them. In love he accepted them, and lifted their vision to the standard of Christ's perfect love.

1. If I speak in the tongues of men and of angels, but have not love, I am a noisy gong or a clanging cymbal.

Besides the languages we acquire naturally, there are others imparted to us by the inspiration of the Spirit. These can be human or heavenly tongues in infinite variety. But whether men recognize them (as at Pentecost), or only heaven recognizes them, the speaker is only a discordant noise if he lacks love. He may use the fullest range of expression, yet he is just a "loudmouth." Loveless language may arrest attention, but it cannot satisfy the heart. Only love can harmonize the gifts we receive. It was this love of Christ which "controlled" Paul (2 Cor. 5:14) and caused him to use the supernatural power given him by the Holy Spirit (1 Cor. 2:4; 1 Thess. 1:5; 2 Cor. 6:3-6) with such great effect.

2. And if I have prophetic powers, and understand all mysteries and all knowledge, and if I have all faith, so as to remove mountains, but have not love, I am nothing.

Even if I exercise a wide prophetic ministry, understand all mysteries, and receive tens of thousands of words of knowledge that flow in a continuous stream, and if through the gift of faith I do all the mighty things that this makes possible, yet lack love, I would still have no real worth in God's sight. He may use me in spite of myself.

Paul never says that without love God's gifts are false, for prophecy, tongues, faith and knowledge remain genuine manifestations. Just as a person may sing or preach without love, he may also bring genuine heavenly illumination, enrichment and deliverance to others. Yet if the *motive* in all this activity is self-interest rather than the building up of the Body of believers, *the person* who expresses the gifts is nothing: "*I* am nothing." Despite his natural and supernatural abilities and theological orthodoxy, he can still exert a loveless influence.

Where a man exercises genuine gifts without love and the compassion of Christ, God may well bless His own word through him. Yet though he may be seen and praised by others, like the hypocrites Jesus mentioned, he has no eternal reward. All that he has, he has received already—the reward of receiving merely human honor, for his heart is barren. Already he has been "paid in full" (Matt. 6:2-5, 16). Lacking love and obedience, Jesus will disown him (Matt. 7:21-23), for he cannot truly represent his Lord (John 14:15; 15:12). In contrast, a gift of tongues, interpretation or prophecy, exercised by a Christian moving in the love of Christ, is a manifestation of exquisite beauty and lasting worth.

3. If I give away all I have, and if I deliver my body to be burned, but have not love, I gain nothing.

Because we find it so easy to look on outward appearances, we may mistake self-sacrifice and even martyrdom as the highest expressions of love. Yet even these may come from a hard and loveless heart or from a desire to attract human attention and approval. Anyone who performs such acts of "goodness" with these motives is not in the least benefited. But love without gifts is not the choice the apostle offers us. Instead, he sees love *with* the gifts of the Spirit as the most excellent way (14:1). Neither gifts nor acts of charity nor martyrdom can be discarded in favor of love. Rather, these express His love, and make it tangible. Jesus wants us to love, not as a substitute for gifts, but as a prerequisite for their effective and acceptable use.

4-8a. Love is patient and kind; love is not jealous or boastful; it is not arrogant or rude. Love does not insist on its own way; it is not irritable or resentful;

**it does not rejoice at wrong, but rejoices in the right.
Love bears all things, believes all things, hopes all
things, endures all things. Love never ends.**

In these verses, Paul holds up before us a portrait of
Jesus, for love reduced to its simplest terms is Christlikeness.
Jesus is love personified. In Him, love reaches perfection.

The Spirit of Jesus never inspires us to exercise gifts
or serve Him in any way contrary to what we find in this
portrait. Jesus is our example. He is our Savior, Master
and Model (1Pet. 2:21).

Love is patient. Love is long-tempered, forbearing, react-
ing patiently when wronged, not losing its temper no matter
what it has to put up with from others. Love's patience
never runs out—even when difficult people both in and out
of the church at Corinth (or in our town) are apt to hurt
tender feelings, or strain relationships. At times it is so easy
to retaliate, or nurse a grievance, or to become bitter and
angry; but love is patient, for it has in it a breath of the
infinite patience of the God of Love. This kind of love is
illustrated in the love of the waiting Father who never gave
up hope (Luke 15:20-24). It was patience such as this that
bore with rebellion, unbelief and ingratitude in the days of
Noah, giving time for repentance until the ark was built
(1 Pet. 3:20). The sole reason why any man is saved is
because God's patience has not run out, for "the Lord is
not slow about his promise as some count slowness, but
is *patient toward you*, not wishing for any to perish, but
for all to come to repentance" (2 Pet. 3:9, NASB; see 3:15).

Love is kind. Love will do good to others, be they kind
or unkind. "It looks for a way of being constructive" (Phillips) even when others are destructive, misrepresent, or don't
understand. There is no place for hardness or sharpness.
Love has a greatness of spirit, for it demonstrates itself
in kindness, helpfulness and selfless giving. Jesus showed
great kindness even to a fault-finding, jealous, scheming

disciple. He was the Good Samaritan who stooped to show kindness to the very ones who abused, insulted and killed Him.

Usually we find it easier to apply "love" in general over the whole world than to relate it to a specific situation and demonstrate kindness to a neighbor in need. But with Jesus, love was constantly demonstrated in His lovingkindness to people around Him: "He went about doing good, and healing all that were oppressed by the devil" (Acts 10:38).

Love is not jealous. Love is not motivated by jealousy when others have received gifts we have not received. Nor does it belittle the good qualities or gifts of others by direct word or implication (James 3:16-18). Love is not envious of another's gifts, opportunities, abilities, possessions, or position. It is not competitive in this sense, but instead rejoices at other people's happiness. There is no rivalry where there is love.

Love is not boastful. Love does not boast and feel proud of its insights, experiences, abilities or position. It does not draw attention to itself nor brag that it is better than others who exercise differing gifts. When it receives undeserved blessings, it is acutely aware that they are given because the Father has graciously drawn us and moved upon our hearts (John 6:44). Since God gives the grace and attracts us to himself, He takes away every vestige of credit for coming, receiving, enjoying, serving. If we boast, we advertise our spiritual poverty in contrast to our Lord. Because Jesus loved, He girded himself with a towel, washed the disciples' dusty feet, and invited them to show love and humility in similar practical ways (John 13:4-17). There is no swagger about such a love. It will gladly witness to what God has done, but boasting is out (Mark 5:19; Rom. 12:3-16)! The humble person is teachable and receptive, submissive to other Christians—"subject to one another out of reverence for Christ" (Eph. 5:21).

Love is not arrogant. The word *phusioō*—itself a noisy

sounding word—means "to inflate, puff up." Love does not "cherish inflated ideas of its own importance" (Phillips). From the Day of Pentecost onward, transformed disciples could startle others with their testimony of a living, personal Christ. They could infuriate with their joy and confidence, and their carelessness as to the effects of their testimony. They could bewilder with their boldness since they knew no fear of men. Yet for all this difference their witness could be a humble one. The Corinthians, however, urgently needed God's corrective, for their desire to excel in the gifts was not motivated by love alone: it was mixed with their own human ambition.

The particular Greek word *phusioō* had been used centuries earlier in Aesop's fable of the frog which blew itself bigger and bigger in an attempt to be as large as a cow. Finally disaster struck with instantaneous deflation! By choosing this descriptive word Paul suggests that conceit is noisy, ridiculous and dangerous.

Love *grows* up: it never merely swells or exaggerates its importance. Love makes men sincere, unaffected, natural and humble, for they are no longer self-sufficient or self-occupied. They are free to be themselves. When we realize that Jesus loves us and we accept that love, the wonder of it produces in us amazement and humble gratitude, not bragging. David Watson writes:

> One of the commonest snares in Christian circles is exaggeration. We talk in glowing terms about the numbers at a meeting, or about the results of a mission, or about some blessings received. At the heart of the problem is a dissatisfaction either with God or with ourselves, or with both. The facts seem too small, so we blow them up, we inflate them! In so doing, of course, we are cherishing inflated ideas of our own importance, and God has often a humbling but effective way of bursting the bubble of our pride. Love is satisfied with God, and satisfied with God's way of working (which may be to humble us!), whether the outward results are impressive or not.[1]

Anyone is arrogant who feels he has all the divine equipment required and therefore has no need of any further charismatic gifts or abilities. He has made more of himself than corresponds to reality. It is all too easy to let such bluff rob us of God's further provision.

In the charismatic context, love does not become arrogant when it receives any of the grace-gifts, because, like the gift of Christ our life, and the gift of the Spirit, it is not of our works, lest any man should take any credit to himself.

Love is not rude. Love neither behaves gracelessly nor tactlessly. It is significant that in Greek, the word for "grace" and for "charm, beauty, gracefulness" is the same (*charis*). God's grace never produces unattractiveness. There can be much uninviting testimony, unattractive witness and plain bluntness in Christian service. The unkind and thoughtless comment preceded by "I believe in saying what I think" (which really means "I believe in saying before I think") is neither beautiful nor becoming. Love is pleasing to behold, attractive, courteous, gracious. Only when we learn to love and prefer one another before ourselves will we lose all self-assertiveness with its accompanying rudeness.

Love does not insist on its own way. It is never self-seeking or selfish (see 10:24). The man guided by love does not demand that others be guided as he feels the Lord has guided him: he is not overbearing, and therefore he does not censure or hold in contempt the spirituality of another who feels no call to act as he has done. He won't use "bulldozer tactics" on another, because he knows his own heart too well to consider that his limited concept of truth and experience is the standard to which others must bow. Even if his own theology were correct, he realizes his attitude must be the same. Love's attitude will allow the development of other sincerely held convictions, while it dedicates itself to the highest for God, knowing that "each of us shall give account of *himself* to God" (Rom. 14:12). In Romans 14, Paul devotes a whole chapter to applying this truth.

Instead of an overbearing attitude, the Spirit produces *gentleness* within the harvest-field of our lives (Gal. 5:23). This gentleness is love's tenderness which will not allow itself to hurt others needlessly. It can exercise its gentleness with the greatest reserves of strength, using only that which is necessary for the present task, like a muscular father who gently holds his new-born baby.

Jesus the Shepherd is the perfect example of gentleness. "Take my yoke upon you," He invited, "and learn from me, for I am gentle and lowly in heart" (Matt. 11:29). A bent bruised reed would not be broken by His hand, nor a smoldering, nearly lifeless wick snuffed out (Matt. 12:20). His strong but gentle touch brought and encouraged life, not death. Little wonder then that Paul could mention this quality when he referred to "the gentleness of Christ" (2 Cor. 10:1). The prophet Isaiah had earlier painted a picture of the loving Shepherd's provision and care for His sheep. The Lord is seen coming with all the might and energy of the universe at His command, but He does not come to terrify or coerce with such power. Instead, He notices all the needs of the flock, and then proceeds to meet them. He is pictured gathering the lambs in His arms and carrying them across His chest, and gently leading those that need tender and understanding care (Isa. 40:10-11).

Paul's words should inspire us to lead and instruct others with this gentle touch, rather than insisting on our own way. Naked strength can utterly bruise and crush the spirit, but strength clothed in gentleness can be direct without wounding unnecessarily, or breaking relationships.

Love is not irritable. Love is not touchy or bad-tempered; "not quick to take offence" (NEB). The Lord Jesus hated sin, but He was never angry or irritated at wrong done to himself. When faced with that, He was serene, not irritable. Whenever people misunderstood or disbelieved Him, or spoke rudely to Him, He never reacted with irritation. When He was reviled, He did not revile in return; when He suffered,

He did not threaten, but met the envy, bitterness, sarcasm and hatred that crucified Him with compassionate love, trusting to Him who judges justly (1 Pet. 2:21-23). And we, like our Lord and example, are called to live not naturally, but supernaturally, with the same divine supply of God's love poured into our hearts through the Holy Spirit given to us (Rom. 5:5). With God-given God-centered love within us, reactions are purified and lifted above touchiness and pettiness, sarcasm and sullenness, irritability and bad temper.

But while love cannot react in such negative fashion, love can be angry. Though God is loving, He has wrath against all ungodliness and wickedness. Jesus could be strong in denunciation and anger. At the outset of His ministry, and again near the end, He revealed himself as the inexorable opponent of all unholy practices in the temple. Those guilty of secularizing and desecrating His Father's house would know His undisguised anger (John 2:13-17; Matt. 21:12-13). And when some, in their hardness of heart, delayed healing because it was not according to their doctrinal timetable, He was angry and proceeded to answer the human need, even though it brought hatred and destruction upon himself (Mark 3:1-6; Luke 13:10-16). There was anger at sin, but no irritation at personal hurt.

Love is not resentful. "It keeps no score of wrongs" (NEB; see NASB) which it has suffered. It records no black mark against another, for it has no desire to retaliate. Love never harbors a grudge nor memorizes injustices, for it has an amazing capacity to forget. The Christian's Master and Example came to blot out our transgressions, and to remember them against us no more (Isa. 43:25; Jer. 31:34), and if we would follow in His footsteps, we cannot take a different way. Jesus keeps no score of our wrongs, for His love involves forgetting as well as forgiving.

Love does not rejoice at wrong, but rejoices in the right. It takes no pleasure in being censorious. "Love is never glad when others go wrong" (Moffatt). It cannot be neutral, for it sides with the truth. Arnold Bittlinger, with true insight, remarks:

> To rejoice at our brother's wrong is natural. For then *we* are seen in a better light. Something is possibly confirmed that we "always knew" to be true. Some opponents of spiritual gifts lie in wait to find a person exercising gifts and behaving like a "traditional Pentecostal," so that their prejudice can be confirmed. Naturally the opposite danger also exists, that some who feel they are the "gifted" ones, rejoice when their opponents fall into slander and lovelessness, etc. Think of how many discussions in Christian circles would lose their fuel, if gossip and back-chat were excluded, and if love became the first law—love that does not rejoice at wrong . . .
>
> "Love rejoices in the right." Whoever is not irritated by others, forgets the evil done to him and does not rejoice in the wrongs of others, will find that his perception of the truth is sharpened. Not only the darkness in the neighbour becomes visible, but also the light. There are areas in one's brother's life through which the truth begins to shine—and love rejoices in this. This not only strengthens the light in one's brother, but also gives one the strength to call unrighteousness by its name when it arises. Only when I am rejoicing in the truth can I pull the beam out of my own eye and the mote out of my brother's. [2]

Yet love not only rejoices *in* the truth: it "joyfully *sides with* the truth" (*sunchairei*) and sympathizes with its advancement. It is not academic nor sentimental, but affirms the necessity for *living, acting and speaking (alētheuō)* the truth in love (Eph. 4:15, TAB). As it is true that faith without love is dead, so love without truth and biblical reality is "flying blind." Jesus is described as full of grace *and* truth (John 1:14).

Love does not mean peace at any price. That can be laziness, self-protectiveness, sentimentality, or a lack of real interest in another's welfare. Love is always eager to accept what is true, and truth in turn will always lead toward Him who is the truth. Love is therefore prepared to consider seriously the views and teaching of men of God who differ from our own interpretation of scripture. Those who have received certain spiritual gifts will rejoice that, while it has never been the ideal, God has greatly used spiritual and able teachers of the Word who have never exercised such gifts of power. Those who have love will praise God for the truth they have received through such people. To close our minds to this fact is to prefer darkness to light and prejudice to truth. Likewise, those without gifts of devotion and power will rejoice that God is fulfilling His promises, and increasingly blessing and using those who exercise these gifts.

Love rejoices in what is true and right. But that is not as easy as it sounds, for sometimes the last thing we wish to hear and practice is the truth. One of the hardest things is to be one hundred percent honest and fair with some aspect of truth when we have traditionally been brought up to see things differently. "Can any good thing come out of that despised town of Nazareth?" To our shame, it may need a miracle of grace to admit the possibility.

No one can ever complain about excesses in the charismatic realm if genuine scriptural worship is not permitted in an atmosphere of love and Christian acceptance. If we refuse the genuine, we actively promote excesses and falsity. Instead of providing a helpful and constructive environment, there is only negativism which breeds a lack of confidence in authority and leadership. This in turn opens the way for the removal of restraint. Love rejoices in the exercise of the genuine: it does not stifle it, but provides an atmosphere of a mutual search for truth, in which we can all learn our lessons, correct our emphases, and be built up. Mistakes may be made here as in other areas of living, but Christian love provides a constructive environment for learning.

Love bears all things. It does not retaliate when wronged

(1 Pet. 2:23), but forgives those who hate and seek to destroy (Acts 7:59-60). It does not carry unforgiveness or criticism within its heart. The word translated "bears" (*stegō*) also contains the further thought of "covering." Love conceals the faults of others (1 Pet. 4:8; Prov. 10:12; Isa. 58:6-7; Ezek. 16:3-14). Rather than emphasize another's lack, love sees what it can do to restore and build. It desires to bring positive blessing, regardless of whether it is misunderstood or criticized.

Love believes all things. This does not mean that love is blind or credulous, or that it is easily deceived, but that it is not suspicious or cynical. Love believes the best about others until it is compelled to accept a contrary verdict. It was because Jesus saw in outcasts hidden splendor and infinite capabilities lying buried that He became the friend of tax collectors and sinners, and His belief in them was undoubtedly a factor in their salvation.

Love provides a positive atmosphere, for it is "always eager to believe the best" (Moffatt), rather than to anticipate and hence encourage the worst. Love helps people become what they should be. There is a strong tendency for people to become what we expect them to be. If we bring a new Christian—or one who has had a moral lapse—or indeed *any* person, into a church fellowship where there is an unencouraging pessimistic attitude, or where there is an expectation of backsliding, this attitude itself will actively encourage failure. Those responsible for this are as much to blame as the individual himself, if he falls.

Jesus knew all the bad but encouraged the good in the woman of Samaria, and sent her back heartened with a message of life, salvation and victory over sin; awakened to new and glorious possibilities (John 4:7-42). To have shown no love and to have expected the worst would only have sown seeds of despair and invited continued defeat.

Love hopes all things. Love is "always hopeful" (Moffatt). It gets no satisfaction from finding faults and blemishes. With God all things are possible, and so we ought never despair over anyone. God can work miracles! He never despairs of us or regards us as hopeless, but continues to work for our good. This is His and love's way of seeking to win another to what is right.

Love endures all things. It remains steadfast to the end. No hardship, discouragement or rebuff can quench it. Natural love does not survive very long when it is not reciprocated. Because it comes from the natural mind and heart, it draws back when offended. But though storms come and trying circumstances prevail, true love continues to trust and rejoice in a God of love.

Love never ends. Love is inexhaustible. It can say in the face of hurts, "Whatever you do, I'll always love you." C. K. Barrett comments:

> If my relationship with my fellowman is soured by his rebuffs, then it is not love; genuine love will always persist.[3]

Love is eternal, for it is the very essence of God himself; it continues on, for it is a foretaste of what we will experience in heaven. Our Lord demonstrated and inspired just such never-ending love in spite of all circumstances (Luke 15:20-24; 23:34; John 15:13; Acts 7:59-60).

> His love has no limit, His grace has no measure,
> His power no boundary known unto men;
> For out of His infinite riches in Jesus
> He giveth and giveth and giveth again.[4]

So we are thrown back to our Lord's life for illustrations of love. There we see love in action

> coming, forgiving, guiding;
> healing, calming, helping;
> revealing, teaching, feeding;
> rebuking, warning, pleading;
> hoping, weeping, waiting;
> persisting, sacrificing, inviting;
> attracting, blessing, rejoicing;
> liberating, inspiring, equipping.

There we see His love convicting of unbelief and sin; accepting a sinful woman's grateful and loving offering; and upholding God's truth against the inroads of pharisaism.

But above all, holy love was at work saving through the dying, rising, interceding and returning Lord.

Truly our Lord's love hallowed, beautified, ennobled and enriched everyone who responded to it. And He is just the same today!

Needless to say, this love (*agapē*) demonstrated by Jesus of Nazareth is no natural kind of love. It is nothing less than the manifestation of God himself, for "God is love" (1 John 4:8). This love is the first-fruit of the Spirit. Indeed, it is the complete harvest of the Spirit (Gal. 5:22-23, NEB) summed up in one word. Either directly or by synonyms (or where a negative is mentioned and a positive is implied), each fruit is included. The total harvest depends on love.

Love is patient—*patience*.

Love is kind—*kindness*.

Love is not jealous or boastful. It is "always slow to expose, always eager to believe the best, always hopeful" (13:7, Moffatt)—*goodness*.

Love is not arrogant . . . does not insist on its own way—*gentleness* (humility, TEV).

Love is not irritable or resentful . . . bears all things . . . endures all things—*peace* and *self-control*.

Love rejoices in the truth—*joy* and *faithfulness*.

If we have love we have the full harvest of the Spirit, for the one word Love embodies the whole cluster of the nine fruits of Galatians 5.

Though the world, the flesh and the devil have terribly marred the human character, in these verses we have a picture of what the grace of God and the power of the Holy Spirit can do in our lives to produce within us the nature of Jesus. "A new commandment I give to you, that you love one another; even as I have loved you, that you also love one another. By this all men will know that you are my disciples, if you have love for one another" (John 13:34-35).

How can we receive this divine love? It is certain that we cannot work it up. Love comes through responding to Jesus and loving Him as Lord. "We love, because he first loved us" (1 John 4:19). The awareness of His love deepens and increases as we love and worship Him and open ourselves to Him for all He desires to give. We find that "God's love has been poured into our hearts through the Holy Spirit" (Rom. 5:5). As we receive this love, our capacity to contain it is enlarged yet further, for the more receptive the heart the more God pours His love into it. Through receiving love from Him we grow in desire to further express it specifically to others in their need. "Beloved, let us love one another; for love is of God, and everyone *loving* has been born of God and knows God. The one *not loving* does not know God, for God is love" (1 John 4:7-8, literal translation). Our love, as God's, is evidenced in specific acts of practical loving. Yet over all we must gratefully acknowledge: "The Spirit produces love" (Gal. 5:22, TEV).

8b-10. As for prophecy, it will pass away; as for tongues, they will cease; as for knowledge, it will pass away. For our knowledge is imperfect and our prophecy is imperfect; but when the perfect comes, the imperfect will pass away.

Prophecy and special gifts of knowledge reveal fragments of knowledge only. They are incomplete and imperfect. Though the other spiritual gifts are not said to be imperfect, they must be included, for they too will all pass away just like the Lord's Supper (see 11:26) when totality—the culmination—comes, and we see the Lord face to face. Arnold Bittlinger writes:

> The gifts will be superfluous when that which is perfect has come. Prophecy will be replaced by a direct entry into the divine will and its secrets. Speaking in other languages

will become superfluous because what was "exceptional" shall become "normal." We shall join in the choir of the heavenly hosts. Words of knowledge will be superfluous when we see God face to face, when we participate directly in His unlimited wisdom. Here on this earth the gifts are imperfect. They are limited by our body, our language, our comprehension, etc. In the gifts we grasp divine reality— but only imperfectly. When Christ returns, the perfect will appear and the imperfect will cease. Then we will see in all completeness that which previously was only partial.[5]

While the gifts themselves are perfect since they are given by the Spirit, imperfect humans exercising them make them —and any other thing they touch—less than they could be. All the time we are in this world we live in the age of childhood and immaturity, and only at Christ's coming will we reach perfect spiritual manhood and maturity.

> **11-12. When I was a child, I spoke like a child, I thought like a child, I reasoned like a child; when I became a man, I gave up childish ways. For now we see in a mirror dimly, but then face to face. Now I know in part; then I shall understand fully, even as I have been fully understood.**

Within this present world, all Christians see dimly in a mirror. Spiritual values are indistinct, with satanic power always seeking to obliterate distinctions between light and darkness, truth and error. Even if we have become more mature in spiritual truth in this world (see 14:20), in the light of eternity we are still children (Eph. 5:1; Phil. 2:15; 1 John 3:7-8), knowing only in part. But this present childhood state will not continue: earthly immaturity will be discarded when we see Jesus face to face. Then we pass into true maturity where there is perfect knowledge and observation of the Master. Perfection will have come. The temporal things belonging to this immature age shall be forgotten, for the eternal realities will have replaced them.

13. So faith, hope, love abide, these three; but the greatest of these is love.

Faith, hope and love all continue.

Faith is looking away from self with grateful, confident continuing trust in God as He is. Faith here and now may waver, but then it will be perfect. In this verse abiding faith is the attitude of complete trust in God and reliance on Him alone.

Hope continues likewise, for even in heaven there will always be a forward aspect, always the as-yet-unrealized splendor, always the opportunity to know more of the glory and wonder of our Triune God. Hallelujah! It will take all eternity to appreciate the eternal state. There will be nothing static in heaven, and none shall arrive at a final position. Though all knowledge will be available to us, it will yet have to be fully appreciated, personally grasped and enjoyed. There shall ever be new vistas apparent to our gaze, ever new desires to serve Him further. There is always more to follow.

Love is not only greater than that which passes, but also the greatest of that which is permanent. It is greater than faith because faith receives, whereas love gives. It is greater than hope because hope is never fully realized. Love, however, is always supremely satisfying. We are satisfied with God's love for us, and satisfied in being able to love God and others. God does not trust (in the sense of committing himself to some other being); neither does He hope, but He does love, for He is love. When men love, they are involved, however imperfectly, in what God is doing.[6]

If we are about to bring any gift (whether natural or supernatural) to the altar, and we become aware of bitterness, unkind feelings, pride, resentment, contempt, jealousy, or lovelessness in any form toward any human being, and especially to those in the household of faith, then we must not present our gift but deal with first things first. We are instructed to go, take immediate steps to be reconciled with our brothers so that love and harmony prevail—and only then come forward to bring our gift to the altar with humility and joy. *Only then* will it be an acceptable offering to the Head of the Church (Matt. 5:23-24; Ps. 66:18), and only then will we have value in His sight.

Paul by no means stands alone in showing the imperative of love. John stressed it (e.g , 1 John 2:9-10; 4:7-10, 16) as did Peter when he wrote to early Christians, linking love and gifts together:

> Above all hold unfailing your love for one another, since love covers a multitude of sins. Practice hospitality ungrudgingly to one another. As each has received a gift, employ it for one another, as good stewards of God's varied grace: whoever speaks, as one who utters oracles of God; whoever renders service, as one who renders it by the strength which God supplies; in order that in everything, God may be glorified through Jesus Christ. To Him belong glory and dominion for ever and ever. Amen (1 Pet. 4:8-11).

3

Prophecy, Tongues and Interpretation

1 CORINTHIANS 14

Prophecy, Tongues and Interpretation:
Their Values and Safeguards (14:1-33a)

Paul has set his hymn of love right in the middle of his discussion on spiritual gifts. He first considered them in general, emphasizing that God has inspired them and has appointed ministries based on them (see 12:4-10, 28). He next turned his readers' attention to the necessity of love, and now returns to consider, in detail, prophecy, tongues and interpretation.

While the Apostle's chief aim in chapters 12, 13 and 14 is to teach how the gifts should be ministered *for the good of all in public worship*, in passing he sheds light on the personal use of tongues.

Because he discusses tongues more than any other gift, and it is the most misunderstood of all God's endowments, we will consider his teaching carefully.

Instead of dealing systematically with tongues, interpretation and prophecy, Paul moves back and forth between them, comparing, contrasting, commending, correcting.

We will see that sometimes principles discovered about one gift are equally applicable to others.

1. Make love your aim, and earnestly desire the spiritual gifts, especially that you may prophesy.

The thought within the Greek (*diōkete tēn agapēn*) is of pursuing love tenaciously. Earlier the Apostle encouraged his readers to desire earnestly the higher gifts (12:31). Now he enlarges on this thought and commands them both to pursue love and to desire earnestly *all* the spiritual gifts. These are not alternatives and we are not invited to state our preference, for if love fills our hearts we will desire any gifts which help us express that love effectively. Even those Christians who were already flowing in the exercise of the gifts were to continue to wait on God for further manifestations.

Both prophecy and tongues are to be earnestly desired, for they are included within the spiritual gifts. Nevertheless, they represent only some of the gifts mentioned in 12:8-10.

Prophecy is of major importance and we are commanded to desire it over and above all other gifts. Paul makes three points: make love (*agapē*) your constant aim; earnestly desire all God's gifts; and of these, desire to prophesy most of all. This word "prophecy," we noted earlier (12:10), is used both in a narrow and a broad sense. Because there is a plurality of *gifts* in the "higher gift" category (see 12:31), prophecy in this verse is best understood in the broad sense covering all the gifts of revelation.

2. For one who speaks in a tongue speaks not to men but to God; for no one understands him, but he utters mysteries in the Spirit.

Speaking in tongues is essentially prayer in which a man speaks to God (14:14, 28). It is something that has meaning, something God understands (14:14-17). Tongues is a communication breakthrough for the Christian—a real aid to worship.

The purpose of tongues is therefore misunderstood if we think of it as a message to people. It is always prayer.

It may be prayer *plus* other factors as on the Day of Pentecost, but the prayer aspect will never be absent.

The Lord can work miracles in communication as in any other sphere, so we should not therefore assume that because a gift involves language it must be what the Bible terms "speaking in tongues." There is ample evidence that on occasions God has given a number of Christians a gift of speaking in entirely unlearned languages *when speaking to men in evangelism*, and through this unbelievers have heard the gospel, or been led to commit themselves to Christ. But we should classify this supernatural enabling as *the working of a miracle in the realm of language*, rather than confuse it with the gift of tongues which is confined to the area of prayer. God can impart a new language for evangelistic or similar purposes, but this is a miracle of communication that has nothing to do with prayer: it is not therefore the gift of speaking to God in tongues as at Pentecost, Caesarea, Ephesus, Samaria, Corinth, and in the life of Paul.

Speaking in tongues involves uttering mysteries in the Holy Spirit. The word *mustēria* used here can also be translated "hidden truths, secret truths, or sacred secrets." In other words, a man's own human spirit inspired by the Spirit enters into these mysteries. The speaker and God are sharing and communicating truth on the level of the spirit.

The term *"unknown* tongues" (KJV) is without Greek support in any of the passages in which it occurs, and is correctly omitted in RSV, for though tongues are always unknown to the speaker, they can on occasion be recognized by those who hear (Acts 2:6-11). Similarly, terms like "tongues of ecstasy" and "ecstatic utterance" in some translations are nowhere in the Greek text, and their introduction to any translation is misleading. The verb *existēmi* is used twice to describe *the hearers* who were "amazed" or "ecstatic" when they *heard* tongues (Acts 2:7; 10:45), but tongues or those who speak in tongues are never described in this way. We should therefore follow the Greek closely and translate simply as "tongues" or "languages." Besides this simple description, other biblical terms are "other tongues" (Acts 2:4), "new tongues" (Mark 16:17), and "various kinds of tongues" (1 Cor. 12:10, 28).

He who speaks in tongues does not speak with an uncontrolled tongue but by a Spirit-controlled, Spirit-inspired tongue. He speaks in or by the Spirit. "He is speaking secret truths by the power of the Spirit" (TEV).

3-5. On the other hand, he who prophesies speaks to men for their upbuilding and encouragement and consolation. He who speaks in a tongue edifies himself, but he who prophesies edifies the church. Now I want you all to speak in tongues, but even more to prophesy. He who prophesies is greater than he who speaks in tongues, unless some one interprets, so that the church may be edified.

Speaking in tongues has spiritual importance and enhances spiritual life and growth. Like ordinary prayer, the Lord's Supper and the Word of God, it is a valuable means of developing the fruit of the Spirit and of building up and strengthening the speaker for more effective service for God. There is great value in being occupied with the Lord, and we cannot commune with Him without being enriched by the experience—whether we are immediately aware of the enrichment or not.

The word *oikodomeó* means "to build a house, repair, construct, establish." When used metaphorically it means "to contribute to the advancement of Christian growth, to edify, stimulate growth, advance a person's spiritual condition, promote the spiritual life." "Edification" suggests something that is architectural, solid, well-founded, orderly, balanced and useful in the Christian's character.

Paul had earlier stated that "*love* builds up, edifies" (8:1): Now he says that *tongues* builds up, edifies, for it repairs the ravages caused by earlier sin and unbelief. This gift is an aid to devotion and a spiritually constructive exercise which brings the Christian's life into greater balance and strength. Praying in tongues, like receiving Jesus as Lord and Savior and following Him, is itself a real act of faith in the promises and provisions of the Lord. *It is part of the Christian's daily faith-walk.* For many today, it represents the greatest act of stepping out upon the word of the Lord and moving at His beckoning since conversion. The writer to the Hebrews reminds us that "without faith it is impossible to please him. For whoever would draw near to God must believe that he exists and that he rewards those who seek him" (Heb. 11:6). God is pleased and rewards every step of faith made on the basis of His Word.

Speaking in tongues among Spirit-baptized Christians is a deliberate act of the will co-operating in faith with the prompting of the Holy Spirit. God promises upbuilding to those who pray in this way, but this only becomes real in our own experience when the word is believed and acted upon. It is through faith and patience that God's promises are inherited (Heb. 6:12). So one of the reasons why continuing to pray in tongues brings enrichment is simply that active faith still inherits the benefits, provisions and promises God has made. If we resist trusting God in any area of His provision, including praying in tongues, impoverishment results. Conversely, any deliberate acts of faith and obedience we make, further stimulate and increase our faith, so that we find it easier to believe God in greater measure.

Having the ability to pray in tongues is not a basis for pride, since the gift is not given in payment for righteous living. It is given to Christians to build them up and help them live holy and more effective lives. *It is therefore a clear sign that the person who exercises tongues has certainly not reached maturity!* The gift is not given to make the pray-er better than others who do not pray this way, but to make him stronger, more balanced and spiritually alive than he was before. A Christian *without* this gift could well be an older, more mature and disciplined Christian in many respects than one *with* this gift. Yet regardless of how advanced he may be, the Lord will increase his strength if he appropriates and faithfully exercises this ability. Because speaking in tongues is a means of communication between a man and his Lord, it establishes new depths of relationship with Him. He is brought to a place where he can more readily worship in spirit and in truth.

In contrast to speaking in tongues, *prophecy involves speaking to men and the church* for their upbuilding, encouragement and consolation. The thoughts behind the word "upbuilding" (*oikodomen*) are, of course, the same as mentioned earlier. But in addition to edification, God's people also need encouragement and consolation, for they are in the forefront of a battle that never lets up. Yet God is in control. He knows and is able to meet our needs. Edification, encouragement and consolation through the gift of prophecy channel God's ministry to His people at their point of need, and give them fresh inspiration and strength.

Speaking in tongues is desirable and Paul wants all his readers to exercise it. Yet at this point he is thinking of tongues as an individual devotional exercise rather than public utterances, as a comparison with other passages indicates (see 12:28; 14:18-19, 26-28).

Although the gift of tongues was abused at Corinth, as were other provisions such as the Lord's Supper, Paul never sought to stop its use anymore than to stop the observance of the Supper. He chose rather to actively encourage its continued expression in God's appointed way.

While speaking in tongues is desirable, and all are encouraged to exercise it, there is a right and a wrong way of doing so. Only if tongues are interpreted do they have a place in authoritative public utterance. But once they *are* interpreted, tongues plus interpretation are as valuable as prophecy in their ability to build up the assembly. They then have the dual function of building up both the church and the individual.

Prophecy is more valuable in the congregation than uninterpreted tongues, since people can understand it directly, and make their response.

Paul envisages the possibility of every Christian prophesying—a theme he takes up again later—and he wants all to do so (see 12:31; 14:1, 24, 31, 39). But although all are eligible to prophesy, only some in the church were called to the recognized *ministry* of prophecy, that is, to be *prophets* (see 12:28-29).

6-9. Now, brethren, if I come to you speaking in tongues, how shall I benefit you unless I bring you some revelation or knowledge or prophecy or teaching? If even lifeless instruments, such as the flute or the harp, do not give distinct notes, how will anyone know what is played? And if the bugle gives an indistinct sound, who will get ready for battle? So with yourselves; if you in a tongue utter speech that is not intelligible, how will anyone know what is said? For you will be speaking into the air.

To listen to public tongues-utterances without interpretation will not profit the congregation. From their point of view there would be much more value in revelation, knowledge, prophecy or teaching. It would be quite possible for Paul himself to speak publicly in his own *devotional* language, but he would not use any gift in a way God had not intended, for this would not help others in a meeting. Anyone who speaks in tongues in public utterance without it being interpreted may as well talk to the winds for all the good it will do the hearers. A bugle can make a meaningless and therefore useless noise, but if a distinct tune is played which is interpreted as a call to arms, the citizens will respond. In the same way, if God wants to call forth a response from the congregation, the people must first understand what has been said.

A hammer is a most effective tool for the purpose for which it was designed, but it is totally inadequate for drilling holes or planing wood. The Corinthians needed to use their new tongue for the purpose God intended, but they also needed to recognize that it is only one of the tools He has designed for the building of the church. Interpretation is another.

10-11. There are doubtless many different languages in the world, and none is without meaning; but if I do not know the meaning of the language, I shall be a foreigner to the speaker and the speaker a foreigner to me.

Tongues are genuine languages with real words which express meaning and can be interpreted (see 14:19). Languages can vary greatly, be sophisticated or primitive, but they will not be just a few ever-recurring syllables. If that happens when speaking in tongues, the gift may be genuine but it has not developed sufficiently. The speaker's faith has faltered before God has finished inspiring the gift. God wants to extend any repetitive language, especially so before He anoints someone to bring a public utterance in tongues.

12. So with yourselves; since you are eager for manifestations of the Spirit, strive to excel in building up the church.

Tongues and prophecy, with other gifts, are manifestations of the Spirit. They express His life. The word translated "manifestations" literally means "spirits" (*pneumatōn*) and refers to the breathings of inspiration and their expression.

In Greek, "spirit, breath, wind" are the same word *pneuma*, a connection which has been frequently taken up in Christian song with hymns like "O Breath of God, Come Sweeping Through Us . . ." and "Breathe on Me, Breath of God." When the Wind of God blows upon and within us it moves and activates. It becomes obvious.

In biblical thought, *pneuma* was alive and had breath, and was a potential source of inspiration. As a living agency it breathed within and brought inspiration and expressed itself in accord with its character. If evil, it inspired evil. If human, it expressed its nature in purely human or natural ways. But the Spirit of God within the Christian had power to breathe into his being *God's* holy breath and so inspire him with revelation. Throughout the Bible, the Holy Spirit is inseparable from divine inspiration and manifestation. [1]

All the gifts are to be used for building up and strengthening others in the fellowship. We can translate: "Since you strive for spiritual gifts, seek that you may abound in them for the strengthening of the church." God wants us to be stimulated and inspired by the Spirit and to co-operate with the Lord in an intelligent, edifying and self-disciplined manner. We are to excel in building up the church.

13. Therefore, he who speaks in a tongue should pray for the power to interpret.

While Paul affirms the use of tongues as a personal devotional exercise addressed to the Lord, in this chapter his main emphasis is on the ministry gifts as they concern public worship and affect others. It is "the church" (14: 4-5, 12, 19, 23), "the other man" (14:17), and the effect of a man's public ministry *on others* (14:6-9) that dominate his thinking here.

In view of the church's need to identify with the public utterances, the one who prays in tongues should seek God for the interpretation. Interpretation is given in response to prayer, though it is not necessarily received by the one who prays for it (14:28). It is not a natural linguistic ability, and unlike human translation, is not produced by the reasonings and accumulated wisdom of the mind.

14. For if I pray in a tongue, my spirit prays but my mind is unfruitful.

On the phrase "my spirit prays," Barrett writes helpfully:

> Paul's language lacks clarity and precision here because he is compressing into a few words the thoughts (1) that it is the Holy Spirit of God that is at work, inspiring Christian worship and prayer; (2) that the work of the Spirit is crystallized into a specific gift; (3) this gift is given in such personal terms to *me* that I can speak of it as *mine*—in short as *my* spirit . . . [2]

The NEB translates, "If I use such language in my prayer, *the Spirit in me prays*, but my intellect lies fallow."

Throughout these verses the thought is so closely interrelated that references to the *pneuma* (Spirit/spirit) praying, singing and blessing can refer either to *the Spirit of God* inspiring the human spirit, or to *the human spirit itself* as supernaturally enabled by the Holy Spirit. But Paul is unconcerned about the ambiguity, for there is always full co-operation between the two when speaking in tongues (Acts 2:4). Without the Holy Spirit the Christian *cannot* pray in tongues, and without the human spirit's co-operation *He will not*.

When using a heavenly language, the speaker's conscious mind is not directly involved in forming words. When Paul prays in tongues he likens his mind to a field which normally is used for sowing or reaping but which is temporarily lying fallow.

Some have seriously misunderstood this text, assuming that Paul describes himself as in a trance-state or beside himself. But this is not so, for Paul describes something superrational, not irrational. It is neither below the level of reason, nor contrary to reason, but beyond its limitations. In tongues the mind of God takes over from the reason of man. Therefore speaking in tongues is *an uplifting act* transcending the ordinary level of rational communication.

The mind is an important God-given faculty and we are to use it in worship (Mark 12:30, 33). There is no substitute for disciplined thought and the Bible makes much of it (Matt. 22:42; Rom. 12:3; 1 Cor. 14:20; Eph. 4:17, 23; Phil. 4:8). God's people are to use their minds with real application (1 Pet. 1:13).

But the life of an individual involves much more than the mind, and in scripture a man's thoughts are not regarded as above reproach. Barrett writes:

> It is evident that the mind is the rational element in man's being, prized by many of Paul's contemporaries as the highest and intrinsically good part of human nature. Paul did not rate rationality so high; the mind is not sinless but needs to be renewed (Rom. 12:2). [3]

Similarly he writes on Rom. 1:28 of Paul's comment that God gave some who were conformed to this age over to a base and unfit mind:

> It may be observed that for Paul . . . the mind is not a higher, divine element in man, or even necessarily good. It is capable of, but it is thereby implied that it needs, renewal. [4]

The Bible speaks of base minds, minds that are hostile to God, hardened minds, minds that are blinded, depraved and corrupt minds (Rom. 1:28; 8:7; 2 Cor. 3:14; 4:4; 1 Tim. 6:3-5; 2 Tim. 3:8).

Even the minds of believers need renewing, for their thoughts can still be led astray (2 Cor. 11:3). Clearly then, believers do not automatically have power to comprehend spiritual values (Rom. 12:2; Eph. 3:18; Luke 24:45). Jesus himself had said, "Out of your inner being (not 'out of your mind') shall flow rivers of living water" (John 7:38).

A man's mind can become a great liability if wrongly used, for it can think up naturalistic reasons for not being entirely God's. It can easily be puffed up and mislead a man into thinking he is bigger than corresponds to facts (8:1-2). It can choose to follow its own wisdom and thought pattern and forget that God's thoughts are higher than ours (Isa. 55:8-9). It has an amazing ability to rationalize. And so the mind, for all its capacity, has very real limitations.

Paul recognized that there was also a language of the heart and inner spirit, where human language is utterly inadequate and a person incapable of expressing himself. Paul's mind placed severe limits on the expression of his deepest yearnings, for he was aware of God-given emotions and promptings in his spirit which transcend all powers of thought (Phil. 4:7; Rom. 11:33-36; 2 Cor. 9:15; Eph. 3:19; 1 Pet. 1:8). And so the mind reaches out, but realizes its limitations, and we sing

> What language shall I borrow
> To thank Thee, dearest Friend . . .

and

> O for a *thousand* tongues to sing
> My great Redeemer's praise . . .

Paul was a highly intelligent man with a keenly trained mind, yet he saw nothing inconsistent in saying that in tongues *his* own mind was unfruitful, or lying fallow. Speaking in tongues provided a method of side-stepping the limitations of his intellect.

When we pray in this way it is beyond the power of the mind to understand or obstruct. The mind is in no way empty. In fact it may be very active, but it is not the source of the utterance. The human spirit is the active element under the controlling intelligence of the Holy Spirit who inspires the words (Acts 2:4).

15. What am I to do? I will pray with the spirit and I will pray with the mind also; I will sing with the spirit and I will sing with the mind also.

The verse can be equally translated, "I will pray by (or 'with') the *Spirit* . . . ; I will sing by (or 'with') the *Spirit*."

To pray with the understanding is essential, but it is only *one* acceptable way of communicating with God. Paul complemented it with praying with the Spirit/spirit—synonymous here with praying in a tongue. He will neither exclude the spirit nor the mind. He will use both his new tongue and his native tongue, for neither removes the need of the other.

It is possible to praise the Lord with songs in our new language, and Paul does that as well. Singing with or by the Spirit is a release of worship and praise which has neither selected verses, set tunes or metre, but a spontaneous expression of tongues in a free-flowing melody. The worshipper is expressing his own worship and praise to the Lord (see Eph. 5:18-19; Col. 3:16). When these individual songs are sung together, they make up a harmonious choir-piece, which rises and falls, ebbs and flows as conducted by the Holy Spirit.

What dimensions of praise still wait to be experienced! For the Lord wants to further sensitize our spirits and lead us into a far higher level of singing with the Spirit than His church enjoys at present. This is another means we have for expressing the true beauty of holiness.

The one who speaks or sings in a tongue is not just a passive instrument under the Holy Spirit: rather he commits himself consciously and *with determination* to the task of having a balanced prayer life: "I will pray with the Spirit . . . I will sing with the Spirit." In other words, we are to pray in tongues when we feel like it and when we don't!

When speaking in tongues, *we* do the speaking. The Holy Spirit never speaks in tongues (see 14:2, 4-6, 16, 18, 27; Acts 2:4; 10:46; 19:6). The supernatural element lies in His providing the language, not in doing the speaking. Praying with the Spirit/spirit or "as the Spirit gives utterance" (Acts 2:4) indicates that the vocabulary, syntax and thought content expressed in tongues are in the mind of the Spirit, and not in the mind of the speaker.

16-17. Otherwise, if you bless with the spirit, how can any one in the position of an outsider say the "Amen" to your thanksgiving when he does not know what you are saying? For you may give thanks well enough, but the other man is not edified.

Again, the opening clause can be translated "if you bless by (or 'with') the *Spirit*."

One purpose of tongues is to praise (*eulogeō* to eulogize) and give thanks (*eucharisteō*) from the inner spirit. (See also Acts 2:11; 10:44-46.)

When our love for the Lord is cool we may feel there are ample English words with which to praise Him. There is no purpose in tongues, for we can get along fine without the gift. It is superfluous. But when Jesus baptizes us in the Spirit all is changed. Faith grows. We feel closer to Him. We are amazed and awed at His grace, love and provision for us. Now we know how little we know, but our awareness of His greatness has expanded and our love for Him is increased, released. Now the heart is fuller than before.

This would normally present a problem, for the fuller the heart the more difficult it is to find the right words in our native language to express all the love, praise, gratitude and adoration that wells up within. The best we can offer is so small. The dictionary proves inadequate and restrictive, for the Triune God is greater than every collection of known words. Somewhat like Solomon we feel "the largest dictionary cannot describe You. How much less these limited words which I have learnt" (see 1 Kings 8:27). If we say God is wonderful, all-glorious, almighty—He is better than that! If we say He is Creator, Lord, Savior, Shepherd, Rock, King of kings and Lord of lords, Divine Physician, Teacher, the Bread of Life—He is far greater than any such description!

Isaac Watts could well sing:

Join *all* the glorious names of wisdom, love and power,
That mortals ever knew, That angels ever bore:

All are too mean to speak His worth
Too mean to set my Saviour forth.

This is one reason why we *need* tongues.

When the river of the Spirit begins to flow and overflow its banks, it breaks out of the confines of customary praise to magnify God in the language of the Spirit. The gift of tongues becomes a vehicle of adoration and worship that glorifies the Lord.

Neither the Christian nor the unbeliever is edified when there is an uninterpreted language, and Paul is highly critical of such a practice. If someone was to give thanks in the presence of outsiders, they could not comprehend or say an intelligent "Amen." It would not help them at all. Those who do not understand must be given every consideration and included as much as possible in meaningful worship. The congregation must guard against moving on to something new before the Spirit's purpose in the tongues utterance is completed through interpretation.

In praising with the spirit, by the Holy Spirit's enabling, the Corinthians were "indeed giving thanks well"—beautifully. The Greek word *kalōs* (an adverb from *kalos*) can be translated as "nobly, worthily, becomingly, well, suitably, in a beautiful way, delightfully." William Barclay writes:

> *Kalos* is that which is not only practically and morally good, but that which is also aesthetically good, which is lovely and pleasing to the eye. . . . *Kalos* adds to the idea of goodness the idea of beauty, of loveliness, of graciousness, of winsomeness. [5]

In God's sight the Corinthians' thanksgiving, prayer and praise in tongues was pleasing and acceptable, though it had no place in public utterance when uninterpreted.

18. I thank God that I speak in tongues more than you all.

The gift of tongues is something Paul is by no means ashamed of testifying to or possessing (see 14:6, 14-15). There is no suggestion that in mock humility he must remain silent about this personal blessing, lest he draw attention from the Lord. That could not be, since tongues actually involve speaking to God and being occupied with Him. Like eternal life, speaking in tongues is a gift for those dependent on His grace and who need His help and provision in their lives.

Quality-wise, the gift of tongues is something given by God himself, something worth thanking Him publicly for, something spiritually constructive, something Paul is personally enthusiastic about, and something beautiful.

Time-wise, tongues was a gift that Paul, the intellectual giant, was using 21 or 22 years after his conversion.[6] This gift is not therefore just for spiritual babyhood or kindergarten, but also for mature saints. Paul was no newcomer to the Christian scene. He was a veteran missionary, and during this, his third missionary journey, he went on record to say that he was still speaking in tongues—and expected to continue to do so in the future. "What am I to do?" he says. "I *will* pray with the spirit . . . I *will* sing with the spirit."

In view of his use of this gift so long after conversion it is clear that Paul felt it was valuable even in the spiritual advancement of an apostle who had seen the Lord, had been granted visions, and who had exercised most if not all of the other power-gifts of 12:8-10. Though this spiritual giant also exhibited the *fruit* of the Spirit in large measure, he still had not graduated out of speaking in tongues, and apparently was not anticipating doing so this side of heaven (1 Cor. 1:4-7).

Quantity-wise, tongues was a gift Paul rejoiced to exercise not merely occasionally but a great deal. It was something he used even more than the Corinthians! What is more, he thanked God that he could use it so often.

Place-wise, it is *in Ephesus* that Paul mentions his current practice of speaking in tongues, for he was there when he wrote these words (see 16:8). Paul thanks God for it, practices it more in Ephesus than they do in Corinth, speaks of it as prayer and praise, testifies to its personal upbuilding quality, and knows that what he commends now while ministering in Ephesus is the mind of the Lord (14:37-38).

As stewards of God's grace, the apostles regarded seriously their responsibility to share any helpful insights committed to them (4:1-2; Luke 16:1-13; Eph. 3:2; 1 Pet. 4:10-11).

Paul spent three years in Ephesus communicating the truth which had been entrusted to him (Acts 20:17-31). Referring to this time, he asserted, "I did not shrink from declaring to you anything that was profitable. . . . I did not shrink from declaring to you the whole counsel of God" (Acts 20:20, 27).

It would be both theologically and psychologically impossible for Paul to live and worship in Ephesus, yet fail to teach about tongues there, when he was simultaneously commending it in an open letter to the Corinthians, and even testifying to speaking in tongues more than they were doing. This would be hypocrisy. Because it was a love-gift from God to His people which enabled them to communicate with Him in a further edifying dimension, it was clearly profitable. Therefore teaching concerning it would be part of the counsel of God which he was responsible for sharing with people everywhere. Paul could affirm: "My ways in Christ I teach everywhere in every church" (4:17).

Yet while Paul was in Ephesus he reminded his readers that there are many other profitable gifts *beside* tongues. Let them therefore be aware of its benefits, but recognize also that the Lord had provided other weapons in the armory of God.

19. Nevertheless, in church I would rather speak five words with my mind, in order to instruct others, than ten thousand words in a tongue.

While the gift of tongues has real value in personal communication with the Lord, it was never intended as a means of public instruction. That was foreign to its purpose. Five intelligible words which could teach others and call forth an intelligent response of "Amen" were to be preferred to 10,000 that no one in the congregation understood. Paul is not saying that always and everywhere, in church and out, in public and in private, it is better to speak with understanding than in tongues. *Somewhere*, Paul spoke in tongues "more than you all," but he would not do this when God's immediate purpose for him was to instruct others.

In this verse Paul's reference is clearly to *uninterpreted* tongues because no mention is made of the further gift of interpretation, and if the tongue was interpreted the people would in fact understand, and experience the same upbuilding as prophecy imparts (14:5). But if uninterpreted, Paul's many words in his Spirit-given language would have *less* value for the congregation than five ordinary words.

Where was the place Paul spoke in tongues "more than you all"? The Apostle does not elaborate, but it would certainly have been in private worship and intercession. Presumably he would also do the same when worshipping and praying with others (Acts 2:1-4; 10:44-46; 19:1-7), but not when he was occupied in teaching the congregation.

Some have suggested that Paul implies criticism of tongues since it "only" builds up the Christian's own soul rather than the Church, and to pray in this way is therefore to be self-centered and indifferent to wider need and ministry. But this is neither logical nor scriptural. (1) If cultivating this gift for self-edification shows spiritual self-centeredness, then *Paul himself* must have been an apostolic monument to an extreme and enthusiastic form of it. (2) It is not selfish but scriptural to "build up *yourselves*" (Jude 20-21; 1 Tim. 4:14-16; Acts 20:32) and to grow in grace (2 Cor. 3:18; Phil. 3:13-14), for then the individual can teach others rather than imposing continuing burdens upon them

(Heb. 5:12). (3) There is no way of building up the Body which does not involve building up the individual units of it. A nation or a congregation is only as strong as its individual members. (4) Even with prophecy, which is usually directed to the larger group all at once, the Body is built up only when the members themselves respond to it on an individual basis. (5) When we are strengthened and made sensitive to the voice of God through praying in tongues, we are more receptive to the prompting of the Spirit to bring *other* gifts which benefit the Church.

20. Brethren, do not be children in your thinking; be babes in evil, but in thinking be mature.

Paul had expanded their vision by reminding them of the wealth of gifts available. He then instructed them to desire to exercise these with discernment, sensitivity and love. Let them co-operate with God's purpose for the gifts rather than frustrate His intention by using them unwisely and lovelessly. They should have little personal knowledge of wickedness, but should use their intelligence to make mature Christian judgments.

21-22. In the law it is written, "By men of strange tongues and by the lips of foreigners will I speak to this people, and even then they will not listen to me, says the Lord." Thus, tongues are a sign not for believers but for unbelievers, while prophecy is not for unbelievers but for believers.

Tongues has the effect of being a sign to unbelievers. The prophet Isaiah had earlier offered the Jews rest and repose in the name of the Lord, but rebellious Israel was set in her ways and would not respond in obedience and faith. So in punishment, God brought upon her the Assyrian invaders whose strange tongues were heard in the land (Isa. 28:11-12). But these same tongues had two distinct aspects:

to the Assyrian victors their own tongues were, of course, joyous in victory; but to the unbelieving, disobedient and vanquished Jews, there was nothing joyous about them! The sound of the invaders' foreign tongues all around was an alarming and convincing sign of God's overruling power and judgment upon them. Similarly within the Christian age, the gift of tongues has two aspects, depending on individual outlook. To the Christian it is a joyous gift of communication, but to the unbelieving it is a sign that Christ's people possess access to a realm of experience with God from which they are excluded. Consequently, it indicated a line of separation and of judgment.

Barrett sees the sign as

> presumably a sign of judgment, as in . . . Isaiah 20:3, the naked and barefooted prophet is a sign of impending doom, of military overthrow and social servitude. When they are not met with faith (cf. Heb. 4:2), tongues *serve* to harden and thus to condemn the unbeliever (cf. v. 23f.); this is not their only purpose (as it was not the only purpose of the parables of Jesus, notwithstanding Mark 4: 11f.), for they also serve to build up the speaker, and, though they do not build up, will at least not offend a Christian assembly that understands what is going on. For this twofold effect of one phenomenon we may compare Paul's use (in Rom. 9:33) of another verse from Isa. 28 together with Isa. 8:14: of the same Stone it can be said that it is a stone of stumbling and a rock of offence, and that he who believes in it (Him) shall not be ashamed. So it is with tongues: the point might perhaps be more clearly put if it were said that they are a sign by which believers are distinguished from unbelievers, since the latter reveal themselves by the reaction described in v. 23.[7]

Prophecy serves as a sign for believers. It demonstrates the power of a contemporary God and signifies that Jesus is risen indeed and moving and inspiring in sovereign grace.

23-25. If, therefore, the whole church assembles

and all speak in tongues, and outsiders or unbelievers enter, will they not say that you are mad? But if all prophesy, and an unbeliever or outsider enters, he is convicted by all, he is called to account by all, the secrets of his heart are disclosed; and so, falling on his face, he will worship God and declare that God is really among you.

The gift of tongues will never be palatable to the natural man or the natural mind, for it is spiritually discerned (2:11-16). No explanations or apostolic examples or teachings are in themselves sufficient to break down the barriers of unbelief and ignorance. Only those who will follow the scriptural teaching and example regardless of their unanswered questions shall know the spiritual reality that can come through tongues. Tongues represent a way of blessing that is only open to those who walk by faith in God's provision. If it makes sense to them, they will follow God: if many unanswered questions remain, they will still follow, for Christians are believers who trust in *God's* wisdom and faithfulness.

If unbelievers or inquirers entered and heard languages without interpretation, it would naturally seem sheer madness. (The reference here, as in verse 19, is to uninterpreted tongues which are unable to speak to the heart or mind of the hearer.) It is sometimes unavoidable that Christians are misunderstood or labelled mad, as were our Lord and Paul (John 10:20; Acts 26:24-25), but this misunderstanding can be minimized if the use of tongues is disciplined. Though the tongues of the early Christians were inspired utterances and a means of extolling and bringing glory to the Lord (Acts 2:11; 10:46), some unbelievers still ridiculed those who prayed this way, and regarded them as speaking unintelligible gibberish (Acts 2:15). In this case it was not the speakers but the hearers who were at fault. Nevertheless, sensitivity and care will minimize misunderstanding.

Though speaking in tongues could be exercised by all

Christians in the congregation, Paul would not have them doing the right thing in an unsatisfactory way. However, there was no hint that their gift was a fraud.

While prophecy is primarily for the upbuilding, encouragement and consolation of believers rather than the conversion of outsiders, it can have a subsidiary evangelistic purpose as hearers are confronted with God. It is therefore a better gift than tongues for securing heart-searching and repentance, since it is directed to men and carries obvious meaning. Those who hear the voice of the Spirit and are convicted when "the secrets of their hearts" have been disclosed are aware of the immediate presence of God and a profound sense of unworthiness. This dominates everything and continues as the one overriding memory. God is alive and He knows all about us!

The term *prophecy* refers here to revelation in general and a word of knowledge in particular. (See comments on 12:10.)

26. What then, brethren? When you come together, each one has a hymn, a teaching, a revelation, a tongue, an interpretation. Let all things be done for edification (literal translation).

Within the worship of the church there must be a place for songs of praise and aspiration (Rom. 15:9; 1 Cor. 14:15; Eph. 5:19; Col. 3:16; James 5:13), systematic teaching, revelatory gifts and tongues and their interpretation. These all have their purpose, but equally each is restricted to check any imbalance and allow opportunity for the full variety to be expressed. Yet variety in itself does not automatically bring edification. The human motive behind the gift must be right and the individual spirit open and submissive, to allow God's purpose of edification to be realized.

27-28. If any speak in a tongue, let there be only two or at most three, and each in turn; and let one interpret. But if there is no one to interpret, let each

of them keep silence in church and speak to himself
and to God.

Tongues are under the speaker's control. There is absolutely no compulsion to speak out. Each person under the
Spirit's prompting can choose to speak or to refrain, and
also choose the time to speak. Just as a believer can stop
and start speaking in an ordinary language, and can have
complete control over the volume, so it is with tongues.

Tongues place a solemn responsibility upon the one who
uses them publicly. They are for conditional and disciplined
use in church. *Only* if an interpreter is present—which can
be himself (14:13) or someone else—may two or at most
three bring a public utterance. If there is no one present
who has previously interpreted, and the speaker in tongues
has himself never done so, he is to keep silent in public
utterance. Yet rather than suppress the Spirit's moving, he
should pray quietly in tongues in a way that will not inter-
rupt the meeting.

These verses must be understood in the context of early
church worship where the level of life and enjoyment of
the Lord was such that the congregation as a whole frequently
participated in praise and acceptance of the Lord's ministry
to them (14:16, 24-26; 12:3b; Eph. 5:19). We misunderstand
this worship if we think of it as centered around a sole
speaker while the rest sat in complete silence throughout.
So the believer can whisper his adoration and love to the
Lord in his new language without causing a disturbance.
Equally, he can pray in tongues with the prayer flowing
inaudibly from his spirit. As well as stopping confusion, the
assembly's time will not then be wasted. (The phrase "speak
to himself and to God" refers to tongues, for if he had something to share in the language of the congregation it could
be spoken publicly.)

It follows that one who speaks in tongues will learn from
the application of this principle, to distinguish between the
anointing for public ministry and the God-implanted desire

to pray in tongues for personal edification only. Some of his training in faith and sensitivity to the Lord and others will come from this. If he is teachable, yet mistakes the anointing, he will learn from the experience, for his faculties are "trained by practice to distinguish good from evil" (Heb. 5:14). In the loving fellowship and discipline of the church he can be accepted and taught.

After the public utterance of tongues, a solemn responsibility rests upon the individual whom God wants to use in interpretation. Is he walking in the will of God and in love with his brethren? Is he sensitive to the inner voice of the Lord?

Everyone who interprets has done so for the first time. Therefore we should discover whether the Lord is wanting to use someone new instead of one already experienced in this gift, for the interpreter may be *any* Spirit-filled believer. Each should pray, "Lord, am I to be used, or some other?"

So it may not necessarily mean that the tongues-speaker is wholly responsible if interpretation is not given, for it is possible to receive enlightenment without passing it on. However, while the whole church must accept its share of responsibility, if one whom the Lord anointed to interpret failed to do so, the ultimate responsibility remains with the tongues-speaker who would then be given the interpretation. Later, if in an atmosphere of love and understanding someone confesses to receiving the interpretation, but for various reasons did not speak it out, the situation becomes a lesson to the individual and to everyone present. Pride, insensitivity or timidity in an individual can sometimes block the genuine inspiration received. However, through humbly sharing, confessing and receiving the understanding of others in the Body, his acknowledged mistake "works together for good with those who love him" (Rom. 8:28). In this way, everyone becomes trained by practice.

When tongues are brought in public utterance, the church

is responsible for providing a time for seeking the Lord, so that He will give the ability and the anointing to interpret (see 14:13).

In our personal communication with the Lord in tongues, interpretation is unnecessary, and fellowship with the Lord is not affected by its absence.

29-30. Let two or three prophets speak, and let the others weigh what is said. If a revelation is made to another sitting by, let the first be silent.

Prophecy requires the careful attention of all the believers present, and then judgment must be exercised upon it, for prophecy, and even recognized prophets, must be subject to the discernment the Spirit gives to the congregation. In this gift, as in every other, God and man co-operate, but because the human element is fallible, we are to test all that claims to be revelatory truth (1 Thess. 5:19-21). No message must be accepted uncritically.

Revelation from God will always be in harmony with the authoritative and inspired writings (2 Tim. 3:16). In addition, it will honor and exalt the Lord Jesus Christ either directly or indirectly (John 16:13-15). If it clashes with basic truth, or if the truths are right but the spirit is wrong, those waiting on the Lord must discern the mind of the Spirit to bring correction so that God's people may continue to receive true comfort, strength and encouragement. The healthy challenge in Jeremiah against false prophets is needed:

> I did not send the prophets, yet they ran; I did not speak to them, yet they prophesied. But if they had stood in my counsel, then they would have proclaimed my words to my people (see Jer. 23:16-22).[8]

Prophecy can be counterfeited, or a seeming prophetic utterance can be just a product of the *human* spirit. Like knowledge, it is imperfect (see 13:9). All who prophesy must therefore be humble, understanding and sufficiently concerned for the health of the Body, to subject their prophecy to the judgment of others. The true man of God welcomes judgment (John 3:20-21; 1 John 1:6), for the Spirit within him makes him wise and open to reason (James 3:17), and ready to acknowledge his fallibility. At best, he is aware that, like all else, his prophecy and knowledge are only partial (13:9-10).

Prophecy, then, is to be uttered in public so that others can discern. Its message is not to be restricted in any secretive way, for then the Body cannot fulfill its function and weigh the message (Acts 11:27-30). Bob Mumford writes wisely:

> Beware of anyone who has a "word from the Lord" to speak to you in private. A legitimate word of directive prophecy can come to you through a friend, but ask your friend to speak it openly where others can judge.[9]

There can be no true prophecy unless the Holy Spirit gives a definite revelation. The Greek word *apokalypsis* refers to an uncovering or unveiling of that which is normally hidden from sight.

Prophecy and various other gifts are not permanent spiritual endowments which can be exercised at the will and whim of the recipient. If we prophesy once, we do not thereafter "possess" or "have" the gift of prophecy, though we may well be used some other time, or many times in this way.

It follows that prophecy is something different from preaching. It is not a carefully prepared discourse, valuable though that should be.

Even prophecies through recognized prophets must, like tongues, be strictly limited in public worship. No more than two or three who hold prophetic office may speak in any one meeting, and if another Christian receives a revelation, the prophets are to be silent and make room for him to participate. In this they will be obeying the injunction to "do nothing from selfishness or conceit, but in humility count others better than yourselves" (Phil. 2:3; see Rom. 12:10).

The Holy Spirit may wish to present a fresh truth by a further revelation and through someone else. He is the only one able to determine and revise the proceedings during worship to bring the ultimate in blessing, and He must be allowed to do so. Those who are not prophets, yet who receive such a revelation, have the "right of way." This encourages those with a less conspicuous ministry. Any of these can prophesy as long as they do so in turn.

31-32. For you can all prophesy one by one, so that all may learn and all be encouraged; and the spirits of prophets are subject to prophets.

Prophecy is one means of learning. Though it is not produced by the human mind, it *feeds* the mind of the worshippers. In this way all may learn and be encouraged. God's truth is invested with new life, power, freshness and relevance as the Spirit applies it to our situations.

Prophecies and tongues are under the speaker's control, and the person can choose when to speak or whether to speak or refrain. The man is always in control of the inspirations ("spirits, breathings"): the inspirations do not control the man. In practice, this means no one can bring confusion or disorder, and then say, "I couldn't help myself: the Holy Spirit made me do it," for these inspirational outpourings are the spontaneous but gentle breathings or promptings of a God of grace and love, who expects the believer to bring them into the worship in divine order. At no time does the Holy Spirit ever rob a man of his *self*-control: instead, He produces it (Gal. 5:22-23; Prov. 25:28). The responsibility for the exercise of any gift therefore remains fully upon him.

Recognized prophets are also not above the command to orderliness. They too must wait until a suitable time is reached, and then tell out what God has revealed to them. Though they have a genuine revelation from God, if the need arises, they can stop and let another start. The Spirit, we remember, came as a dove, to alight gently upon the Anointed (Luke 3:22). The only coercion He uses is the coercion of love, *for the manifestations of the Spirit are voluntary responses, not involuntary reactions.* Consequently, inspiration cannot be an excuse for refusing to submit to the divine rules laid down.

Consider some of the practical situations in which we are in control of the inspirations.

What can we say about the times when we are certain we have a genuine message from the Lord, yet we get no opportunity to express it; or we have a message without the anointing to bring it forth; or the message simply fades away?

Don't be alarmed! There may be various reasons for this. The Lord may have undoubtedly given a true revelation and equally withdrawn it. We can then learn to say with Job: "The Lord gave, and the Lord has taken away; blessed be the name of the Lord" (Job 1:21).

The revelation we had may be for a future meeting. At that moment it may be to prepare our own hearts, but in a few weeks' time the Lord may give the necessary anointing and opportunity to bring it forth. Or it may come to test our dependence on the Spirit. Am I going to wait for His permission to bring it, or am I going to give it in any case?

Or the Lord may give the message without the anointing repeatedly over a period of weeks or even months to allow the message to become even more part of us, so that our confidence and authority are built up for the precise moment He decides upon. Then we receive the anointing, and the message is given.

Again, there may be no opportunity or anointing to bring His message because the Lord meant it solely for our own personal edification and encouragement.

33a. For God is not a God of confusion but of peace.

If there is any confusion or disharmony, God did not bring it. Arnold Bittlinger wisely notes:

> A charismatic meeting for worship cannot be ordered and controlled by some wooden scheme or formula. Order results when all the members listen to the one Spirit and when each member regards the other as better than himself (Phil. 2:3). Then the result is peace, dynamic orderliness.[10]

33b-36. The Ministry of Women in the Congregation

These verses raise a new subject which is considered separately in the author's forthcoming book, *Experiencing the Holy Spirit*.

37-40. Concluding Instructions

If any one thinks that he is a prophet, or spiritual, he should acknowledge that what I am writing to you is a command of the Lord. If any one does not recognize this, he is not recognized. So, my brethren, earnestly desire to prophesy, and do not forbid speaking in tongues; but all things should be done decently and in order.

All that has been said about love, tongues, prophecy or other gifts and practices, their values, limitations and uses, are not to be ignored as unimportant, for the teaching comes with divine authority. Paul has not spoken from human bias: he has been guided by inspired revelation, and his words represent the *Lord's* command. He has been God's mouthpiece. Jesus himself would have given identical instruction. He, in fact, gave it! Paul could make no higher claim to inspiration. Because of this, to disregard the value of any of the gifts or the necessity of love is to disregard the Lord who gave them. This is equally so if we fail to correct any abuses of these holy gifts and graces.

"If anyone does not recognize this, he is not recognized." If a man claims to have the truth, yet disagrees with Paul or refuses to correct abuses, his "inspiration" is not recognized by Paul. It is false teaching and does not come from God.

Some, and possibly most, in the church had prophesied before (1:7; 12:10, 29; 13:2, 9; 14:3-5, 24, 29-31, 37), but everyone is exhorted to desire earnestly to prophesy. For however many times the gift has been manifested previously, every prophecy must be freshly inspired. We are still entirely dependent upon sovereign grace for further revelation.

Suppression of tongues is not God's method of correcting any abuses. The word *kōluō* (forbid) is also translated "to hinder, prevent, withhold, keep from, withstand" (Matt. 19: 14; Acts 8:36; Luke 6:29; Acts 27:43; 11:17). This phrase could therefore be amplified to read: "Do not forbid or hinder or prevent or withhold or keep from or withstand speaking in tongues."

Possibly a number of the Corinthians were beginning to overreact to the misuse of the gifts. A faction may have been developing there like one in another church, for in Thessalonica they were quenching the Spirit and disturbing the fellowship by despising prophesying (1 Thess. 5:19-21). Forbidding or despising the gifts of the Spirit of holiness is divisive. It destroys edifying, holy and united fellowship. Paul himself corrects and regulates speaking in tongues, but he never hinders its proper use.

Jesus spoke out strongly against those who opposed God's purpose, and bound men with restrictions that would not stand the divine test: "Woe to you lawyers! for you have taken away the key of knowledge; you did not enter yourselves, and you *hindered* [kōluō] those who were entering" (Luke 11:52).

So in Corinth, fleshly reaction to the abuses, and prohibition rather than training, introduced a loveless domination which sought to prevent this expression of worship and praise. But, though it must be seen in its relationship to other gifts and to love, the ability to pray in a God-inspired language was a gift from the Spirit to be recognized, honored and practiced.

Like everything else involving the work and worship of God, all the gifts are to be exercised in a decent and orderly manner. The Greek word for *decently* is a rich one which can also be translated "becomingly, gracefully, honorably, with beauty." The Greek word for *order* refers to "orderliness, arrangement, symmetry." The believer's worship, as his life, needs to be well regulated and open to the orderly arrangement of the living Spirit, for the orderliness He brings is not the orderliness of the cemetery, nor human orderliness, but the orderliness of joyful, growing spiritual life, which moves and flows with ever-changing variation at the inspiration and direction of the Spirit.

We must come under the searchlight of these words and listen to what they say. What is there which irritates and brings discord? Is there unnecessary noise that obtrudes, so that genuine seekers cannot dissociate from it and meet with God? Is there an automatic response of praise, a preoccupied participation with little depth? Is there unreality that disturbs other worshippers? Are overtones of the flesh hindering sensitivity to the Lord and to each other? Are gifts being manifested for self-glory, with mixed motives, or purely for God's glory and the true instruction and upbuilding of His church? Are those who express these gifts disciplined in waiting for the right moment in the flow of the service to share them? Are they waiting for the Spirit's anointing to deepen and increase, so that the life their utterance ministers will also deepen and increase? Are leaders giving adequate instruction and direction in these areas, and with love and gentleness, exercising their God-given authority to correct, teach and exhort—and where necessary to discipline, so that the Body is not hurt nor the Spirit grieved? Are we so content with that which is good that we fail to seek or give opportunity for that which is highest and best? Is it obvious that our public worship is the overflow of hearts that know and love regular fellowship with the Lord in the secret place?

To do things becomingly and with orderliness, in the context of these verses, refers, of course, not to an ordering *without* charismatic worship, but an ordering where the operation of the Spirit's gifts is assumed, commended, inspired, and regulated for the common good. For all things to be done decently and in order requires that they be *done*, not left undone!

Disorderliness comes when the church is out of divine order—when gifts are manifested without divine control. But a church is also disorderly when there is no expression of spiritual gifts at all. It may seem orderly by traditional human standards, but it is out of divine orderliness.

God's order may be evident when all is hushed with a sense of His presence. But His order may also be evident, on occasions, when humanly speaking the situation seems chaotic. When the 120 simultaneously praised God in at least fifteen different languages, some ridiculed them as drunk. Yet this was the genuine, divinely ordered ministry of the Spirit. Later when Ananias and Sapphira were involved in deceit and pride, God dealt with them in severity, seeming to create startling disorder and disturbance of the status quo—but this was God's order (Acts 5:1-11). With Philip's evangelistic ministry, there was loud crying and upheaval as Satan was forced to release his hold, but what was disorderly by human standards was in keeping with people being liberated from demonic power (Acts 8:7; 16:16-24). Yet whatever the outward appearance of the Spirit's ministry, there is need for sensitivity to Him so that all may flow in the accomplishment of His ultimate purpose: then, even out of moments of apparent chaos can come the beauty of wholeness, orderliness, harmony and peace.

Important as are all these aspects in these three chapters of Paul's letter, no doctrine, nor experience, nor gifts, nor even love, has the preeminent or exclusive place. All are meant to demonstrate that "Jesus Christ is Lord," and point to Him.

4

The Continuing Ministry of Jesus in Acts

Jesus revealed to His disciples that He would return to them, not in bodily form, but in the Spirit. The Holy Spirit was to be so like Jesus that Jesus could say to them: "I will not leave you desolate; *I* will come to you" (John 14:18). The Spirit would bring the whole Christ back to the people in all His miracle-working power, authority and perfection of character.

The disciples had been taught that the Spirit would be Jesus' "other Self" (*allos*, John 14:16). He would be "*another* Counsellor," taking Jesus' place and continuing His work.

Jesus had always ministered supernaturally when He was present in body, and His disciples would expect Him, through the Spirit, to continue to do the same work in similar power and graciousness. In this they were not to be disappointed. The mighty works He began on earth (Acts 1:1) would continue in the same way after His ascension, but now individual believers would be empowered by the Spirit of that same Jesus who "went about doing good and healing all that were oppressed by the devil" (Acts 10:38). They would be His hands, eyes, ears and feet (1 Cor. 12:12-27).

As we move through the book of Acts, we see how the Spirit's gifts were prompted and motivated by love and compassion that arose spontaneously from hearts in touch with Jesus. These gifts were an expression of the mind of Jesus—knowing, understanding; the hands of Jesus—caring, healing; the life and voice of Jesus—convicting, inspiring, renewing, and giving hope: all for the common good.

When God moved in the early church, He so enlarged the spiritual capacities of ordinary men and women that they were able to perceive and appropriate in an increasing measure the Lord Jesus himself, and therefore express more of His life, love and power. Accordingly, He received increasing glory.

Some consider that, whereas the Word of God edifies, supernatural acts are without lasting spiritual effect. They are like the glitter and trappings on a Christmas tree, impressive, but useless.

But this is clearly not so. In the early church, the word and the demonstration of the power of the Spirit went together, and people were not asked to choose one or the other. There were indeed those who *would not* believe even if someone should rise from the dead (Luke 16:31). They deliberately resisted truth both seen and heard, and their hearts became hardened as a result, for belief has always been linked with the heart and will of man as well as the head. Yet many, as we shall see, heard God's Word, saw His power, and responded.

In this and the following chapter, attention is drawn to the more conspicuous or "miraculous" demonstrations of the Spirit's presence, and on texts that highlight this emphasis. But God works mightily in silent unobtrusive ways as well as in the spectacular. The limitations of language present us with a very real problem in communicating these two ideas. If in trying to make a particular thought clear we must on occasions refer to the "non-miraculous, regular, usual, or natural" elements of our faith, we are using inadequate modes of expression, because nothing God does can be strictly described as natural, regular or non-miraculous.

If on the other hand we refer to the "miraculous, super-natural, unusual, dramatic, exceptional, spectacular," we are still not being accurate, for what human beings regard as extraordinary is natural to God. Again, some aspects of a believer's life which have by God's grace become natural are startling and remarkable to those who have no personal relationship with Him. The gifts that were described by non-Christians as extraordinary became the wonderful but routine provision of a loving God for His people. What was originally extraordinary for the early church soon became "supernaturally natural."

While we fully recognize the inadequacies of language in this realm, probably the most satisfactory way is to refer to the gifts of the Spirit as "gifts of power" or "gifts of special power" (see comments on 1 Cor. 12:8-10). Where other words such as "miraculous" or "non-miraculous" are used, the reader will appreciate that no words are completely suitable.

As the risen Jesus continued and broadened His ministry to the world, the threefold expression of His life became evident in the church. *His character* was expressed in Christian love and the fruit of the Spirit (1 Cor. 13; Gal. 5:22-23); *His power* was demonstrated in the gifts of the Spirit (1 Cor. 12:4-11); *His authority* was wielded through the ministry gifts of Christ (Eph. 4:11).

In this chapter we will consider the accounts of the supernatural in the book of Acts, and note the positive and negative effects these demonstrations produced.

2:1-4. The Coming of the Spirit

On the Day of Pentecost God suddenly intervened in a transforming way as He touched the 120 disciples (see 1:15). There was a sound from heaven, tongues as of fire, and those who had been unfilled and uninspired moments before were suddenly filled with the Spirit. Where inspiration and power had been lacking there was now abundant life in the

Spirit, and out of this new life came a speaking in other tongues as the Spirit gave them utterance.

Unbelievers soon heard the sound and gathered together where they could overhear spontaneous praise being offered to the Lord. He was being magnified in the congregation of believers (see Ps. 34:3; 35:18; 71:22-24; Luke 2:13-14; Rev. 4:6-11; 5:9-14). With the arrival of the audience, the recital to God of His mighty works had become a recital before men of God's praise.

All were amazed and perplexed at what was taking place, and reactions were varied. Some ridiculed what they could not understand. Others were attracted by the revolutionary change and the obvious dynamism in the disciples, and stayed on to hear Peter preach in the Aramaic language. And the message they heard, reinforced as it was with prophetic revelation, brought conviction, and three thousand were converted and added to the Church.

On this occasion, before Peter had brought any evangelistic message and this great ingathering took place, he and 119 other consecrated Christians—all thrilled with their new life in Christ—had been heard worshipping the Lord in tongues, and this became a powerful factor in the interest and conversion of the multitude.

2:43-47. Many Wonders and Signs Were Done Through the Apostles

No details are given of which gifts were in operation. Yet probably there was the same wide variety as we observe elsewhere in Acts as the living Christ, now resident in the apostles, continued to go around healing many who were under satanic oppression. Bodies, minds and attitudes would have been healed, and faith confirmed and strengthened. Combined with the miracles, the Christians continued ordinary sharing, partaking of the Supper and worshipping. As a result of their varied witness, many more surrendered to the Lord and were added to the Church.

3:6—4:22. From Lameness to Leaping!

When the lame man was healed, there were far-reaching consequences. For the man himself, the effect was twofold: he was perfectly restored to health and to the status of a useful citizen. Then recognizing that his healing had come from God, he praised and glorified Him with an enthusiastic and grateful heart. His life had been transformed and silence had become impossible!

This healing and testimony instantly captured the people's attention. They were filled with wonder and amazement, and we can be sure they listened carefully to Peter and John.

The apostles for their part quickly disowned their own human power as the source of the transforming miracle, and the way was opened to testify to the name and authority of the crucified and risen Jesus of Nazareth who had been with them and done this sign. Everyone saw clearly that Christ's power was not restricted to His work before the crucifixion, for by the Spirit's power He was still active in their midst. With the grateful man standing with Peter and John as visible confirmation of this, many more believed in Jesus and glorified God for what had happened.

But the same miracle had an entirely different effect upon the Jewish leaders. They reacted with annoyance and alarm, realizing that their authority was undermined by yet another expression of God's power through Jesus. So Peter and John were arrested—but were paid the supreme compliment of being identified as followers of Jesus. The leaders might continue to be influenced by emotional considerations against Jesus and His message, arising from the jealousy within their hearts, but such illogical arguments were no longer convincing, for the healed man remained as a devastating testimony to the power of Jesus' name (4:14-16).

4:29-31. Accompaniments of Infilling

The miraculous shaking of the house and the conscious infilling with the Holy Spirit with its new enabling for service resulted in the word of God being delivered with added boldness. Jesus was on *their* side!

4:33. Great Power and Great Grace

These words emphasize that God was demonstrating His power and grace in ways that were meeting people's needs. Only a short time before, the Christians had asked God to "allow us, your servants, to speak your message with all boldness. Stretch out your hand to heal, and grant that wonders and miracles may be performed through the name of your holy Servant Jesus" (4:29-30, TEV). The gifts now manifested with great power were part of the answer to this prayer. No doubt they brought healings and gave increased confidence in the apostles' testimony.

5:3-11. Where Lies Cannot Live

Here the operation of the word of knowledge is recorded. The inmost thoughts of Ananias and Sapphira were laid bare. They had been deliberately deceitful by falsely claiming that the money handed over to the church was the total payment for their land. The uncovering of their lies was followed by two miracles of instantaneous death.

God's intervention in this dramatic way caused great fear to come upon the whole church and on everyone else who heard of these events. Pretence and hyprocrisy were dangerous, for God was well aware of any pretended self-surrender and halfhearted commitment.

5:12-14. More Signs of the Living God

"Now many signs and wonders were done among the people." Again this does not detail the nature of each happening, but the signs and wonders created a holy awe so that no unbeliever dared join the Christians unless he was sincerely repentant. All could see that Christianity was not some new popular movement merely interested in swelling its ranks. Many, however, who sincerely desired to put God first were added to the Lord, and the apostles were held in high honor within the community.

5:15-18. Blessing and Persecution

Numerous people were healed of sickness and delivered from unclean spirits. Not only was God glorified by their release from bondage, but also through the praise, worship and service which the former captives were now able to offer.

Negatively, God's intervention stirred up bitter jealousy within the religious leaders who now seethed with desire to quench every trace of revival. If spiritual gifts could be stopped, the most obvious demonstrations of Jesus' power would be blocked and everything would settle down nicely with no threat to their priestly authority. So the apostles were arrested and imprisoned.

5:19-42. God Needs No Key!

Prison doors were now thrown open, the apostles led out and given directions by an angel of the Lord. Bars and locks were no barrier to God!

After their release, the apostles promptly returned to the temple court and resumed their teaching. But their deliverance immediately alarmed the Jewish authorities. Prison doors had never before proved so futile! This miracle provided increased opportunities to witness to Jesus, but it also brought more persecution. Yet in spite of this, the disciples were in no way deterred. They rejoiced to be identified with the sufferings of Jesus, while continuing their teaching and preaching. They knew that the Lord accompanied them, and this confidence was obvious everywhere they went.

6:8-15. Stephen—Worker of Miracles

"Stephen, full of grace and power, did great wonders and signs" and spoke with "wisdom and the Spirit." Whether we are to understand this latter phrase as referring to the word of wisdom, or God-given wisdom in general, makes little difference, for his ministry was supernatural and rang with authority and truth. However, people who will not believe refuse to do so on emotional or moral grounds rather than on intellectual ones (see John 5:40; 7:17), and this case was no exception. Light was rejected, resistance stiffened, and false charges concocted against Stephen. But his very captivity gave him opportunity to declare that God's purpose of true spiritual worship is made possible only through the Lord Jesus Christ.

7:55. A Glimpse of God's Glory

Stephen's new infilling with the Holy Spirit as he stood before his captors was accompanied by a vision of the glory of God. This brought great encouragement, confidence, and real confirmation that in spite of opposition he was in the center of God's plan. As he gazed, Stephen described the vision to others and used it to underline the truths he had already shared. Jesus was alive and standing in the place of acceptance and authority with His Father: "Behold, I see the heavens opened, and the Son of man standing at the right hand of God." But this revelation which had such a positive effect within Stephen's own heart produced anger and rage in others, while Saul reacted with hatred. Saul himself no doubt recalled the vision many times in the days which followed and was haunted by unresolved questions concerning it. Certainly years later, the memory of Stephen's radiant witness and the guilt of his own involvement remained indelibly printed on his mind (see 22:20).

8:5-8. Proclaiming Christ Through Miracles

The people of Samaria heard Philip proclaiming Christ. "They heard him and saw the signs which he did. For unclean spirits came out of many who were possessed, crying with a loud voice; and many who were paralyzed or lame were healed."

During our Lord's ministry, preaching and expelling evil spirits went together (e.g., Mark 1:32-39). Sometimes the deliverance was marked by screaming (Mark 1:26): other times there was no such display. And now this same ministry of Jesus had been delegated to His followers. They were His Body with a Spirit-implanted desire to minister as He had done. Because He had moved in power upon them, they in turn could know His enabling, and say: "The Spirit of the Lord is upon me, because he has anointed me to preach good news to the poor. He has sent me to proclaim release to the captives and recovering of sight to the blind, to set at liberty those who are oppressed, to proclaim the acceptable year of the Lord" (Luke 4:18-19).

All this supernatural activity captured the attention of the multitudes, who listened carefully to Philip's message. The result was spectacular, and so many responded and were touched by God's miraculous power that the city resounded with joy.

"Proclaiming Christ" (*kērussō*) was linked with supernatural intervention. This proclamation came through *hearing the message* Philip preached, and *seeing the message* in the accompanying signs. So in both ways Christ's power and authority were declared and demonstrated. Word and manifestation were linked in sharing the Good News.

8:14-24. Delay Before Receiving the Spirit

The evangelistic work in Samaria was marked by the Spirit's verification of Philip's ministry by accompanying signs and wonders. Many believed his message and were baptized "in the name of the Lord Jesus" (see 19:5).[1]   In other words, as they were baptized, the name of the Lord Jesus was spoken over them in recognition that they had become His property. By submitting to baptism they "signed themselves over" to Him, and gladly acknowledged that He was their new owner.

But although they were now baptized believers, for some reason they did not receive the Holy Spirit. And the Church was immediately aware of the deficiency. They had *only* been baptized in water, and the Holy Spirit "had not yet fallen on any of them." "They had been baptized into the name of the Lord Jesus, that and nothing more" (8:16, NEB).

It is clear that neither belief, nor belief and baptism, nor "much joy" in the new believers were sufficient evidence that the Holy Spirit had been given. How then did anyone know that the Samaritans had *not* received the Holy Spirit? The only possible explanation is to be found in the absence of supernatural manifestations. F. F. Bruce is surely right when he asserts:

> The receiving of the Holy Spirit in Acts is connected with the manifestation of some spiritual gift.[2]

Since Pentecost, many had been converted and received the Spirit. But in every case, there must have been extraordinary signs, additional to belief, baptism and joy, or the Samaritan position would not have been clearly seen as deficient, and the apostles' intervention would not have been required. No one claimed that these believers must have received the Spirit unconsciously. And when Peter and John came they made no attempt to question the Samaritans' repentance, baptism or sincerity, or convince them theologically that they had in fact already received the Spirit. In spite of belief and Christian baptism, Peter and John (and Luke who records the events) were certain that the Holy Spirit "*had not yet fallen on any of them.*"

God could and did vary the order of events and the timing. He could deliberately delay the reception of the Spirit after belief and baptism (see also 19:1-6), or impart the Spirit upon belief but before baptism (10:44-46). There was no reason to believe that God is imprisoned within a theological system which makes variations impossible.

Some suggest that God deliberately withheld the Spirit because the centuries-old rivalry between Jew and Samaritan might otherwise persist in Jewish-Christian and Samaritan-Christian factions. There may be truth in this suggestion. On the other hand, there were many other methods capable of bringing Jew and Samaritan together. God did not find it difficult to pour out His Spirit obviously and convincingly upon Cornelius and others (10:44-48; 11:21-24), and He could have publicized His complete acceptance of the Samaritans in the same way. Or, by either a voice from heaven or a vision (Luke 3:22; 9:34-36; John 12:28-29; Acts 10:11-16) He could instruct both Jewish and Samaritan Christians to accept one another as full brothers. Yet although we are not told why the reception of the Spirit was delayed on this occasion, the *fact* of the delay is undeniable.

This postponement in the Spirit's coming at Samaria was probably the first occasion after Pentecost when believers did not receive Him to the apostles' satisfaction at baptism. So the apostles dispatched Peter and John to the Samaritan converts. And after they had prayed and placed their hands on them, "they received the Holy Spirit" in a recognizable experience.

While the nature of this obvious manifestation is unspecified, it is clear that the Spirit's descent was linked with definite and acceptable signs. It is implicit within this passage and in line with evidence elsewhere that the gift of tongues was present, for the word *logos* in verse 21 can much more naturally be rendered: "You have neither part nor lot in this *speaking* (or 'word, utterance, speech')." [3] Unlike the others at Samaria, Simon had no part in this God-inspired utterance, for his heart was not right before God. By translating *logos* as it is usually rendered, this verse would then most naturally refer to speaking in tongues in which the firstfruits of worship were offered to the Lord.

All this supernatural activity caused varied reactions: Simon observed that the Spirit was indeed given on this occasion through the laying on of the apostles' hands, and desire erupted within him for the authority and prestige to produce the same effects. He was impressed by the obvious manifestations which came when the Spirit was given. But there was something wrong. Greed and a desire for personal acclaim were in his heart and made him offer the apostles money that he might share their secret. His fleshly desires were in no way crucified with Christ, and so he could not receive or minister His power and life. Peter's reaction was very sharp: "Your silver perish with you, because you thought you could obtain the gift of God with money! You have neither part nor lot in this speech, for your heart is not right before God. Repent therefore of this wickedness of yours, and pray to the Lord that, if possible, the intent of your heart may be forgiven you. . . ." (author's translation). And with this, Simon was terror-stricken lest the power which he had coveted would now be directed against him.

The whole event is a solemn reminder that the Holy Spirit and His associated gifts are not for sale. They are only received humbly through sovereign grace.

8:26-35. Led by the Lord

Two divine commands were given to Philip by direct revelation: through an angel (v. 26) and by the Spirit (v. 29). These enabled Philip to be in the right place at the right moment, while the prophecy of the suffering Servant was being read by the Ethiopian. And as Philip witnessed to the prophecy's fulfillment, his new friend was enabled to make his own intelligent response to the Lord Jesus Christ. He was baptized and then went on his way rejoicing. Tradition says that he returned to Ethiopia to evangelize his own country.

Confirmation of the dramatic nature of the reception of the Holy Spirit in New Testament times is found in the interesting "Western" text which reads, "The Spirit of the Lord *fell* upon the eunuch and the angel of the Lord caught away Philip." But, as F. F. Bruce has noted,

> Even if the best attested text does not explicitly speak of the eunuch's receiving the Spirit, this is probably implicit in the statement that *he went on his way rejoicing.*[4]

8:39. Heavenly Transportation

"The Spirit of the Lord caught up Philip; and the eunuch saw him no more. . . . But Philip was found at Azotus." Evidently Philip was caught up in much the same method of heavenly transport that was experienced by Elijah (1 Kings 18:12; 2 Kings 2:16), the disciples on the Sea of Galilee (John 6:21), and possibly Ezekiel (Ezek. 3:12-14), for Philip next found himself at Azotus, where he continued in his task of preaching the gospel.

9:3-19. Paul—Arrested! Blinded! Filled!

Paul's conversion was a major miracle involving many supernatural incidents. There was the brilliant light, his fall from his horse at the release of divine power, the voice of the Lord from heaven, and his blinding. Later, even before Ananias was told of this, Paul received a vision in which the name "Ananias" was given him, and he was shown that this unknown man was to be the human instrument in the return of his sight. For his part, Ananias was also prepared by a vision and conversation with the risen Lord.

When Paul was initially filled with the Spirit, he was instantly healed of blindness. So we see that the filling was linked in time with at least one miracle.

We cannot say with any certainty that this was when Paul first spoke in tongues, as there is no mention of it in the text. But while dogmatism is impossible, the evidence for it is very strong. When the gift is first mentioned in connection with him, it was obviously an established part of his normal prayer activity, but we have no explicit reference as to when he first received it.

However, the following factors support the belief that Paul first spoke in tongues when Ananias prayed for him. Obviously there must have been a first time when Paul began praying in this way, and his personal Pentecost in which he was initially filled with the Spirit would be the most likely occasion, and be in keeping with the pattern of initial fullness in the lives of the 120, Cornelius and his friends, the Ephesians, and implicitly, the Samaritans (Acts 2; 10; 19; 8). The coming of the Spirit is also the time linked with the initial outpouring of gifts in Joel's prophecy concerning the new age of the Spirit (Joel 2:28-29; Acts 2:17-18, 33). So there was no more likely time to be initially released to worship the Lord in tongues (see note on Titus 3:4-6 in next chapter).

All these miraculous accompaniments of Paul's conversion and his infilling produced world-shaking consequences which the Lord has used for the enrichment of the whole of Christianity.

9:33-35. "Get Up and Make Your Bed"

Aeneas who had been bedridden for eight years, paralyzed and constantly dependent on the help of others, was now healed by God's power and given the opportunity to help and minister to others. And all the residents of Lydda and Sharon saw in this healing such evidence of the power of Jesus that they turned to the Lord. The drawing power of the miracle together with the testimony and preaching of the Christians won immediate response.

9:36-43. The Dead Are Raised to Life

When Dorcas was raised from the dead in answer to Peter's prayer, people saw that Christ's power was not only available for spiritual needs but was also present to renew and restore physical life. Through this, many more were brought to trust in the Lord.

10:3-43. God's Grace Reaches Gentiles

In a vision, Cornelius was instructed to send for Peter and he was given clear directions of where to find him. The next day when Peter was hungry, God gave him a vision of the menu He had prepared for him—a mixture of clean and unclean animals, reptiles and birds that he was to kill and eat! This mixture he must now assimilate! Peter was at first confused—as well he might be—for he, a Jew, had been completely closed to the thought of eating anything that was ceremonially unclean. Now, however, the vision so impressed itself upon his mind that when the men arrived and presented themselves to him, he understood what God was saying, and the once intolerable idea of receiving hospitality and food from a Gentile had ceased to be a problem.

The Lord's revelation to Cornelius prepared his heart for Peter's message, and also made his friends receptive when Peter stood up to preach Christ to them all.

With Peter, the vision and the voice caused in turn perplexity, obedience, confirmation of God's word, hospitality to be extended to Gentiles, and the transformation of his outlook by the then new and revolutionary understanding that God shows no partiality.

10:44-48. Gentiles Receive the Spirit

When the Spirit was outpoured upon the Gentiles His coming was accompanied by speaking in tongues which brought a release of worship and further glory to Jesus Christ. F. F. Bruce comments:

> Apart from such external manifestations, none of the Jewish Christians present, perhaps not even Peter himself, would have been so ready to accept the fact that the Spirit had really come upon them.[5]

Further, the reception of the Spirit evidenced by speaking in tongues convinced Peter that since the Lord had fully accepted them, these *Gentiles* could be baptized as Christians without needing to become circumcised first. The fact that the Holy Spirit "fell on them just as on us at the beginning," plus the roof-top vision, was to provide Peter with the clinching argument at a later point of theological crisis (see 15:4-29). He was able to justify the Gentiles admission to the Church, silence the opposition, and cause all to glorify God together for His grace. God was teaching the Church mighty truths by both word and miraculous confirmation.

11:19-24. The Hand of the Lord Was with Them

In a momentous step forward, unnamed new Christians from Cyprus and Cyrene took the initiative and launched into preaching Jesus as Lord, not this time to Jews or to a Gentile household, but openly to the large Gentile city of Antioch. Until now, breaking new ground in evangelism had been initiated only by apostles or their representatives (such as Philip), but this was a new spontaneous development, a major breakthrough. And as they went out, driven by love and compassion for others, and shared the good news of salvation through Jesus, the Lord was with them and confirmed their message as He stretched out His hand in signs and wonders.

The phrase "the hand of the Lord" describes the obvious and powerful touch of God upon the people (Acts 4:30; 13:10-11; Ezek. 1:3; 3:14, 22; 8:1-2). The Lord was confirming the evangelism by many signs (Mark 16: 20). Then Barnabas came, saw all these evidences of God's grace and rejoiced at His endorsement.

If the apostle Peter had earlier needed to be convinced that God had accepted Cornelius and his fellow Gentiles, then Barnabas—who was not one of the original apostolic band—would have required at least equal confirmation that these new Gentile workers or their converts carried God's authenticating touch upon them. The familiar manifestations of the Spirit linked with faith completely satisfied Barnabas on one of the most important occasions in the history of the Church.

11:27-30. Prophecy Leads to Practical Support

Agabus was inspired by the Spirit to foretell coming famine, and this was taken seriously by the Christians. God was warning them and desiring to use them to bring help and relief to their brothers in Judea.

12:6-17. Miraculous Release

Peter's release from prison involved various supernatural elements, such as the appearance of an angel, a shining light, the blow on Peter's side, the voice and the opening of the gate. By this mighty intervention, God testified eloquently again of His power and concern for His followers.

What wonderful worship, praise and thanksgiving must have taken place in Mary's house that night!

12:21-24. Herods Do Not Live Forever

Herod's death when an angel struck him warned everyone that it is dangerous to receive men's adulation when it belongs solely to God. The touch that had liberated Peter (v. 7) and slew Herod came from the same mighty God! The results of the miracle were probably typical—some would believe and turn to the Lord, while others would rationalize that it was a coincidence which would have occurred in any case!

13:9-12. Teaching by Word and Deeds

The false prophet Elymas was dramatically confronted by the power of God when the Apostle challenged his authority! On this occasion when Paul was filled with the Spirit there were three gifts of the Spirit demonstrated in quick succession. First, the gift of discernment of spirits brought insight that the problem was basically demonic, and Paul reacted with stern authority: "You son of the devil, you enemy of all righteousness, full of all deceit and villainy, will you not stop making crooked the straight paths of the Lord?"

While the problem had a demonic cause, Elymas for his part had deliberately identified himself with opposition to the Lord, and had hardened his own heart. His desire and will were joined with Satan to cause others to deviate from the straight paths of the Lord, and Paul had no hesitation in holding Elymas responsible for his co-operation with the evil one.

Discernment was followed by a word of knowledge which revealed what God was about to do: "And now, behold, the hand of the Lord is upon you, and you shall be blind and unable to see the sun for a time." With this pronouncement the way was opened for the further gift of the working of miracles. Because Paul had complete faith in the word God had given him, and spoke it out, immediately mist and darkness fell upon Elymas and he went about helplessly seeking people to lead him by the hand. Truly, the word of God was living and active and sharper than any double-edged sword!

One important result of this event was that the false prophet's defeat was obvious to all and he had no alternative but to cease opposing God's work! On the other hand, the proconsul saw the word of the Lord confirmed. It was very obvious that the message he had heard was truth indeed! And with this realization, this prominent intelligent man trusted his own life to the Lord.

After the account of these grace-gifts, Luke writes: "Then the proconsul believed, when he saw what had occurred, for he was astonished at *the teaching of the Lord.*" Here the word "teaching" (*didachē*) denotes much more than the spoken statement of truth: it included the miraculous demonstration of God's knowledge, wisdom, love and power.

14:3-4. Signs and Wonders at Iconium

The Lord bore witness to the word of His grace, "granting signs and wonders to be done" by the hands of Paul and Barnabas. But these words and deeds of grace were by no means universally accepted, and the city was split into two factions. Some sided with the Jews, some with the apostles, and finally the two men were forced to leave town.

14:8-10. From Handicap to Wholeness

The crippled man who was healed at Lystra was an incurable case, as Doctor Luke emphasizes. He could not use his feet, he had never walked, he was deformed from birth. But Paul detected by the Spirit that the Holy Spirit had implanted faith within the man's heart so he commanded him to stand. And as he sprang up in obedience he was instantly healed.

This miracle provided further opportunity for preaching the Word, but again fierce opposition was aroused. The Jews, and then those who had so recently regarded Paul and Barnabas as "gods," turned against them.

14:19-21. God's Power Is Greater

Paul, whom the Jews regarded as their most dangerous enemy, was now severely stoned, dragged from the city, and left for dead. But when the disciples gathered about him in prayer, he was miraculously raised up again, and apparently from then on suffered no ill-effects.

15:4-29. Declaring All the Lord Had Done

While this chapter is mainly given over to a crucial debate on theological questions rather than narrative, it is noticeable that Paul and Barnabas declared to the Church Council "all that God had done with them." First, Peter reminded them of the Spirit's outpouring upon the Gentiles—an outpouring which had been evidenced by speaking in tongues.

Then, in greater detail, Paul and Barnabas informed them of the signs and wonders which God had done as they ministered among the Gentiles.

Here we see again how signs and wonders were used by the Christians as important and relevant teaching mediums. Because only the Lord could move miraculously in such a God-exalting fashion, the manifestations were confirming evidences of His approval and blessing. In fact, the gifts were God's own hand, stretched out to heal, help and save. The presence of tongues demonstrated that the Gentiles were just as acceptable to God as the Jewish brethren. God's power was revealed both in word and in obvious deeds—and it was now among Gentiles! Similarly, these and other gifts taught the *Jewish* Christians that if they were not to be left behind while God moved on, they must fully accept those whom the Lord had obviously accepted! The Father of all was still continuing His work among them, welding His family into unity.

16:6-7. A Change of Direction

As Timothy and Paul continued their missionary journey, the Holy Spirit gave them definite instructions not to proceed as they had planned. This guidance may have come through revelation by some unnamed prophet or an ordinary member of the Body of Christ, by a revelation in word or in vision, or by an unmistakable inward prompting of the Spirit.

16:9-10. A Vision in the Night

A new vision was given to Paul, and the words "Come over to Macedonia and help us" were supernaturally impressed upon his mind. God's next purpose for their ministry was now clear.

16:16-25. Satan Loses a Staunch Supporter

The gift of discernment of spirits and the deliverance of a demon-possessed slave-girl had profound effects. The words the girl had spoken were completely true, but the evil spirit inspiring the utterance was a "spirit of divination." Having discerned the spirit behind the testimonials she had been expressing, Paul spoke to it and commanded it to come out of her in the name of Jesus Christ. Upon this command, it obeyed, released its hold upon the girl, and she was set completely free. Satan had lost again!

The doctrine of deliverance has always been unpopular with the devil and with those who remain his willing captives —and also, as in this case, with the men who had vested interests in the girl. Her freedom robbed the slave-owners of their evil source of gain and led to the arrest, beating and imprisonment of Paul and Silas, who were the human cause of all the uproar! However, what seemed like defeat became overwhelming victory as the bruised apostles sang and worshipped in spite of their captivity. Other prisoners overheard their praise, in fact, they could not avoid hearing it! Pain and confinement obviously were powerless to diminish the prisoners' joy, peace and assurance. Here was a new demonstration of power! The power which took authority over demons was completely adequate for the suffering and stress that Paul and Silas were now experiencing.

16:26-34. A Shaken Jailer Comes to the Lord

A sudden earthquake shook the prison foundations, swung open the doors, and snapped the prisoners' fetters. Their restrained reactions to this sudden freedom then gave Paul the opportunity to introduce Jesus to the jailer and all in his household, and the response was overwhelming. All believed, rejoiced in God, and were baptized!

18:9-10. Strengthened to Fight Again

While Paul ministered at Corinth, the Lord spoke to him in a vision. Its message completely reassured and comforted him, for God promised full protection and enabling while he remained there. This gift of loving encouragement undoubtedly strengthened his resolve to go forward without fear.

19:1-7. "Sealed with the Holy Spirit"

When Paul finally moved on to Ephesus, he found a group of about twelve disciples. Their Christian knowledge was defective, but they seem to have been regarded as Christian disciples ("converts," NEB), rather than disciples of John the Baptist.[6] When Paul asked them, "Did you receive the Holy Spirit when you believed?",[7] it is clear that he thought they were Christians. But they had never even heard that there was a Holy Spirit who could now be received by believers. To say the least, their Christian experience was tragically incomplete. Some have the theology without the experience, but these had neither the theology nor the experience.

Yet what is far more important than whether these Ephesians were already Christians *before* Paul met them is that Paul now spoke to them about Jesus and corrected whatever deficiencies still remained in their understanding of the gospel (v. 4). Then after this teaching—which they clearly accepted—Paul was happy to baptize them. Thus at this point they were believers who had heard and responded to the full Christian message.

Now their condition was regularized—with one exception: the Holy Spirit had not come upon them in the accustomed way, and so the matter was not allowed to rest. It did not occur to Paul to inform them that since they had now been fully instructed in the gospel by an apostle and had believed and been baptized with full apostolic approval, they already possessed the Holy Spirit. Instead, just as Ananias had done with him (9:17-18), Paul now fulfilled the same ministry to them when he laid his hands upon each in turn. And as he did so, "the Holy Spirit came on them" as had happened 25 years earlier upon the Church at Pentecost (Acts 2:4, 17-18). Again the gifts of the Spirit were present.

While these twelve Ephesians had known only a brief

lapse in time betwen their baptism as believers and laying on of hands, the difference in that time in their spiritual condition was absolutely crucial. It was the difference between *not* having the Holy Spirit (to use Luke's mode of thought) and having Him come upon them with the manifestations of tongues and prophecy.

With this experience these Ephesians were ushered into full Christian initiation.

But they had only begun! This was just their entry into a new realm of worship and service for the Lord. Now as they went forward bearing Christ's reproach, they would have the enabling of the Spirit which had been missing earlier.

19:11-20. Extraordinary Miracles

During Paul's ministry at Ephesus, various mighty signs and wonders took place. Extraordinary miracles of healing and deliverance were performed through the use of pieces of material that he had touched (Mark 5:27; 6:56). Besides these miracles, the more regular method of deliverance was employed by Paul. The phrase "in the name of Jesus" was noted and seized upon as a magic formula by the seven sons of Sceva who sought to imitate Paul's ministry, but with disastrous results. "And the man in whom the evil spirit was leaped on them, mastered all of them, and overpowered them, so that they fled out of that house naked and wounded."

Evil spirits were a force to be reckoned with, and could speak and act through the one who was possessed. This event illustrates the danger of presumptuously resisting them. They know whether or not a man has God-given authority to challenge them. Those who were present during this incident were filled with awe at the reality of the forces of darkness and the overwhelming power of the name of Jesus. Because of this episode, fear came upon the Jews and Greeks, and the name of the Lord Jesus was extolled. Many new Christians saw firsthand that they could not trifle with the power of Jesus, so they came and confessed their magic practices and associations, and demonstrated their repentance by burning any books and charms which would hinder their own or others' Christian walk. A clean break had to be made with all evil associations.

So the powers of darkness suffered defeat at the name of the Lord, and the gospel message triumphed mightily.

20:9-12. Falling Asleep in Church

After the young man Eutychus fell from a third-story window, Luke the physician was fully convinced that he was dead. But through Paul's ministry he was soon raised to life again. This evidence of the Lord's power and compassion brought great comfort to the believers. Jesus cared about Eutychus and would not permit death to hinder God's plan for his life. Instead of sorrows and hopelessness, there was restoration and life, with further glory to the Lord Jesus.

20:23. "The Holy Spirit Testifies to Me in Every City"

As Paul continued his journeying, the voice of the Spirit gave continuing revelations of the afflictions and imprisonment awaiting him. The same Jesus who prepared His disciples for coming persecution (John 16:1-4) was now warning and preparing Paul's heart. We are not told how these warnings came but it was probably through prophets in the various cities, with perhaps some personal revelation given directly to Paul.

21:4. Forewarned Is Forearmed

Through prophecy it was revealed that grave danger awaited Paul at Jerusalem, and because of this, his friends urged him not to continue. They misinterpreted the purpose of the revelations. Yet Paul knew that this information was given to prepare him further for trials and suffering, and not to warn him to hot-foot it out of town! Just as Jesus did, Paul "steadfastly set his face to go to Jerusalem." He was committed to following his Lord!

21:9. Inspired Ministries at Caesarea

As Paul neared the end of his journey to Jerusalem he arrived at Caesarea and went to stay in Philip's house. Philip's four daughters were known for their prophesying, and they may also have received specific prophecies regarding Paul's future at Jerusalem.

The fact that we have not even one recorded prophecy from these four demonstrates that silence does not mean revelations did not occur. Many had an important but only local or immediate significance, and so were not recorded in the written Word.

21:10-11. "Thus Says the Holy Spirit"

The revelation through Agabus the prophet foretelling Paul's arrest and imprisonment was graphically conveyed in deed and word. Again Paul recognized this as a preparation for the days ahead, but he did not falter in his commitment to God's will, even though he was well aware of the cost of his obedience. He was deeply affected by the love and concern of the Christians, but determined to move on, whether this meant life or death.

22:6-16. Arrested by the Living God

After Paul arrived in Jerusalem, he was arrested as had been foretold. He then testified to the miraculous happenings at his conversion.

By relating these experiences, Paul highlights the importance with which he regarded the supernatural elements of his faith. Though these events had long since passed, they still retained their original value as testimony to the risen Jesus of Nazareth who had earlier spoken to him and called him by name.

Paul later repeated this testimony to Christ's risen life as he stood before King Agrippa and assured him that he "was not disobedient to the heavenly vision" (26:12-22).

22:17-21. Marching Orders

During his testimony Paul related an incident not mentioned earlier in the account of his activity in Jerusalem after his conversion on the Damascus Road (see 9:28-30). About three years after this event, Jesus had appeared to Paul again while he had been worshipping in the temple, and instructed him to leave the city before he was captured. At that time, it was not God's will for him to be imprisoned, but instead to begin ministering to the Gentiles.

These revelations had guided and strengthened Paul. But now when his hearers heard him relating them, they reacted with hatred and rage, and again Paul was faced with the prospect of severe punishment. This was only averted as he disclosed his Roman citizenship, which in turn provided a further opportunity for witnessing.

23:11. The Lord Stood by Him

The night following these events Jesus again revealed himself personally to Paul. This time it was to comfort and encourage the Apostle to remain steadfast, and to inform him that He had arranged the itinerary for Paul's trip to Rome! He was not forgotten! Everything was still under control!

The memory of this word sustained and strengthened Paul during the delays and pressures of the next two years.

27:22-26. With Christ in the Storm

As Paul sailed through the terrifying storm on his journey to Rome, a word of knowledge assured him that all on board would be spared, though the ship itself would be completely wrecked on an island. Again the Lord gave reassurance by repeating that Paul was to make his witness before Caesar in Rome. God was continuing to reveal himself through the gifts and to draw the attention of others to Paul's words. As the narrative reveals, all that Paul had been shown came to pass.

28:3-6. Divinely Protected

Soon the people of Malta also had the opportunity to see a living demonstration of God's power. When a viper slid out of the wood that Paul was adding to the fire, and fastened itself on his hand, they waited expectantly for swelling and dying agonies, but to their astonishment he was completely unaffected. God had worked another miracle of preservation for him (see Mark 16:18).

28:8. Healed by the Lord

While living on Malta, Paul had the opportunity of ministering to the sick father of Publius. And as the Apostle laid hands on him and prayed, he was miraculously healed.

28:9-10. Ministering the Love and Power of Jesus

Paul was now completely accepted. The incident with the viper, followed by the healing of Publius' father, encouraged the remaining sick people on the Island of Malta to come for ministry. And when the missionary party finally had to sail, the Maltese people gratefully expressed their appreciation for their healing by putting on board all the necessary supplies. They had seen an unforgettable demonstration of the love and power of Jesus expressed through His people.

Conclusions

In Acts, as elsewhere, gifts are manifested, not instead of love, but through love. Nor is love present without it being frequently expressed in gifts of various kinds. The whole purpose of the gifts is to express the Lord's love and power in a living and relevant way and to reveal further aspects of His goodness and glory. Whether there were many manifestations of the Spirit such as those associated with Paul's momentous conversion, or more "ordinary" miracles such as the healing of the father of Publius, they were granted by a God of love to convict, direct, deliver, comfort and heal mankind. They acted to amplify Christian witness and to attack unbelief and the powers of darkness. Supernatural signs were *always* given for the ultimate strengthening of the Body—or units within that Body—and the glorification of Jesus Christ, the Head of the Church.

Throughout the history of the Church's early expansion, gifts were combined with faithful preaching to bear testimony to the reality of gospel truth. As we noted in Acts 8:5-7, Luke joins these two aspects under the description of "proclaiming Christ." In 13:9-12 three separate spiritual gifts that operated as a weapon against the opposing powers of evil were regarded as a major part of "the teaching of the Lord." And as we shall see in the next chapter, when Paul mentions the evangelistic methods he used wherever he went —methods only occasionally recorded in Acts—he links together the supernatural and the ordinary as inseparable pillars of the gospel: "For I will not venture to speak of anything except what Christ has wrought through me to win obedience from the Gentiles, by word and deed, by the power of signs and wonders, by the power of the Holy Spirit, so that from Jerusalem and as far round as Illyricum I have fully preached the gospel of Christ" (Rom. 15:18-19).

The risen Jesus taught His church through a great variety of spiritual gifts. These were signs which expressed truths about His ascended glory, sovereignty and wisdom; His power and authority over sin, sickness, demons and death; His acceptance of Gentiles; His power to hear, speak, strengthen, predict, guide, know and comfort; to transport

Philip, blind Paul, release Peter, kill Herod, and judge Ananias and Sapphira.

The lesson is clear: proclaiming Christ, teaching, and fully preaching the gospel require much more than a verbal relating of facts, exposition and theology. We should expect the Lord to show himself alive, powerful, knowledgeable and loving through continuing demonstrations of the Spirit. The message in words is essential but it is neither superior nor inferior to the witness of spiritual gifts. Both are necessary to declare the character and multi-faceted grace of the Lord Jesus Christ. Both are necessary before we can learn from the same balanced, biblical teaching program that the early church enjoyed.

We have noted that grace (*charis*) is expressed in a great variety of miraculous ways, but also in the commonplace. Spectacular miracles stand out from a backdrop of "normal" or natural events. For example, the 120 worship the Lord in tongues, but this is followed by Peter speaking in a language familiar to his hearers. There is the multiplicity of distinctly supernatural manifestations in Acts 5 followed by the shortage of material provisions for widows and the more mundane sacrificial supply by fellow-Christians in Acts 6. There is the record of Stephen working great wonders and signs among the people but then giving his anointed message without any dramatic charismatic overtones (Acts 6:8; 7:1-53). There is the vision granted to him but also the stoning which brought hurt and death while completely in the will of God (7:55-60; see 1 Pet. 4:19). There is the killing of James at the hands of Herod, yet the miraculous release of Peter soon afterwards (12:2, 6-11). Years later, according to tradition, he in turn was finally martyred by being crucified upside down.

In the midst of the miraculous, the Christians devoted themselves to the regular disciplines of teaching, fellowship, breaking of bread and prayers (2:42). They lived for Christ, but there was a price to pay in comfort and material security, for they were arrested, beaten and persecuted (4:2; 5:40; 8:3; 16:19-24). Yet the very persecution which scattered them, also lifted their spiritual horizons to the yet unevangelized regions (8:4; 11:19).

Many of the same people who had seen extraordinary miracles of healing and deliverance (and who knew of the greater power manifest in Christians than in the sons of Sceva) came in "ordinary" acts to confess and renounce their wrong practices and make their peace with God (19:11-20).

Paul who won obedience from the Gentiles "by the power of signs and wonders, by the power of the Holy Spirit," also preached, taught and made his defense in non-miraculous ways (Acts 17:17-31; 22:1-21; 24:10-25). For three years in Ephesus he did not cease to admonish the Christians with tears (20:31). He also appealed to Caesar on the basis of his rights as a Roman citizen (25:11-12). Though mightily used by God in ministering the gifts of the Spirit, this did not usually bring ease. He knew all too well the beatings, lashings, stonings, shipwreck, dangers of many kinds, toil and hardship, sleepless nights, hunger and thirst, cold and exposure, and all the pressures which went along with his high calling (2 Cor. 11:23-28). His ministry of signs and wonders was balanced by reasoned and Spirit-anointed theological teaching in his epistles, and his joy in God was never far removed from much suffering for Christ.

There were many more occasions than those Luke records, where the gifts were in operation within the early church. For example, Luke compresses Paul's eighteen months public ministry in Corinth into eighteen verses (Acts 18:1-18), and mentions only one distinctly supernatural visitation—a private vision given to Paul. Yet when Paul later refers to his ministry there, he says, "I was with you in weakness and in much trembling; and my speech and my message were not in plausible words of wisdom, but in demonstration of the Spirit and power, that your faith might not rest in the wisdom of men but in the power of God" (1 Cor. 2:3-5; see 2 Cor. 12:12). Luke records only really significant examples where some new or unique advance or development took place.

So the Acts presents us with a balanced message which prepares us for disciplined service, fully involving the ordinary and the extraordinary, the non-miraculous and the miraculous, the dramatic and the regular. However, as we noticed earlier, all such terms are inadequate, and represent our human attempts to categorize and describe the differences that exist in God's dealings with men. We must bear in mind that though there is always a mighty spiritual purpose in the more obvious demonstrations of the Spirit, the silent experience of the new birth—of a soul regenerated— is equally miraculous and more eternally life-changing than any other visible miracle.

Blessed be God our Savior!

5

The Continuing Ministry of Jesus in the Epistles and Revelation

The forward move of the Spirit affected every believer and fellowship by bringing the life of the risen Christ within the reach of all. The book of Acts demonstrates this. The Epistles and the Revelation bear the same witness and greatly enlarge our knowledge of the Spirit's work.

The church at Corinth was well endowed with the Spirit's gifts. But just suppose that it had been one of *few* centers where these gifts were originally manifested . . .

Corinth was the capital of the Roman province of Achaia, built on a strategic isthmus between the Saronic Gulf on the west and the Corinthian Gulf on the east. In such a position it was inevitable that it should grow to be one of the greatest and richest commercial centers of the Mediterranean world. It became known as "The Bridge of Greece," and traders and travelers moving from north to south, east and west, stayed there before moving on.

But more important to Paul than commerce, Corinth was a center from which the gospel, once planted, could quickly radiate forth. As the moving population came in contact with the Christians there, many were converted, filled with the Spirit, and became involved in fellowship, worship and the operation of spiritual gifts. Then they in turn went home to spread the news and tell what great things the Lord had done for them.

As well as the movement of these new Christians from Corinth back to their homes, there was the advance into fresh areas by other noted believers such as Aquila and Priscilla, Silas and Timothy (Acts 18:5, 18-19), who traveled extensively sharing the full gospel message of salvation through Christ.

Thus, because of Corinth's place on the trade routes, and its proximity to so many important places, other Christian congregations were soon aware of the Spirit's activity there. If a visiting Christian saw or exercised gifts of the Spirit there and was instructed to desire further manifestations, it would create an impossible theological situation if these gifts could not be exercised back home among his own congregation. Therefore, even apart from convincing scriptural testimony, logic demands that supernatural gifts must have been given to other congregations as well.

Gifts were the Lord's provision for the *universal* church (1 Cor. 12:28). Their purpose was to benefit Christians everywhere (1 Cor. 1:2). Yet non-Christians were also helped as their attention was arrested and they saw God's power demonstrated before their eyes.

Jesus made His promise universal and timeless when He said: "*He who believes in me* will also do the works that I do; and greater works than these will he do, because I go to the Father" (John 14:12). The term *erga* (works, deeds) refers to the numerous miracles, healings, deliverances from demons, signs and mighty acts of power by Jesus (Matt. 11:2, 5; John 5:20, 36; 9:3-4; 10:25, 32; 14:10-12; 15: 24). It meant the multiplication of food supplies, control of the elements, walking on water, and turning water into wine. Our Lord's words were therefore not a promise of *spiritual* works alone, for Jesus accomplished both material and spiritual works for the blessing of men.

The only limitation Jesus placed upon this promise was to confine it to *believers* through whom the power of His risen life was flowing.

Gifts are not always recorded. Difficulties in this or any other area of church life (such as the Lord's Supper) were sure to attract attention and invite correction. But once gifts were matters of common knowledge, accepted, and operating smoothly, there was usually no need to refer to them, because they now formed a regular and healthy part of the church's life. If any comments were necessary, the merest allusion was sufficient to show that the writer had them in mind.

In the pages that follow passages have been arranged in accordance with their generally accepted chronological order. In this way we can see how the Spirit's gifts continued undiminished. Some references are specifically to the Holy Spirit and to the presence of His gifts. Others are more general but have been included because they are fully consistent with the presence of the Spirit's endowments.

1 Thessalonians (c. A.D. 48)

1 Thess. 1:5. Our gospel came to you not only in word, but also in power and in the Holy Spirit.

Though the gospel had, of course, been preached verbally, it was not merely a matter of words. Side by side with the presentation of the truth there was living power to transform lives and situations. This was evident in dynamic operations of the Spirit, no doubt similar to those recorded in Acts (see Rom. 15:17-19; 1 Cor. 2:3-5).

1 Thess. 4:8. God . . . gives His Holy Spirit to you.

The present tense emphasizes that the Spirit was being *continuously bestowed* on the Thessalonians (Gal. 3:5). The book of Acts details how the Spirit was given with real evidences of His coming and activity. Now as Paul writes to the Thessalonians eighteen years after Pentecost, he confirms that the same pattern was continuing, for they were still experiencing fresh outpourings of the Spirit's life and power. The signs were continuing to accompany those who believed.

The clause "His Holy Spirit" mentioned here literally reads, "the Spirit of Him, the Holy (One)," and serves to emphasize both the majesty and the holiness of the Spirit.

> **1 Thess. 5:19-20. Do not quench the Spirit; do not despise prophesying, but test everything.**

To "quench" means to dampen down or restrain.

We can quench a fire as effectively by neglecting to provide more fuel as by dousing it with water or stamping it out. In other words, we can snuff out the Holy Spirit's life by closing our hearts to His touch or simply by ignoring His gentle promptings. Then the isolated fire can only die. Similarly, determined and willful opposition to His activity has the same suffocating effect. It deliberately obliterates the glow of His life.

This verse can also be translated, "Do not quench the spirit"—that *breath of inspiration* which initiates and sustains the expression of divine power, and is related to the Holy Spirit (1 Cor. 14:12). The New English Bible translates: "Do not stifle inspiration," while Knox says, "Do not stifle the utterances of the Spirit." Paul is obviously referring to the gifts of the Spirit listed in 1 Cor. 12:8-10.

The Apostle wants the Thessalonians to be sensitive to the Spirit's life-giving and inspiring breath. His influence in any age can be quenched by ignoring the commands to desire His gifts, by criticizing or repressing them, or by that selfishness—sometimes parading as spirituality—which does not love enough to seek God's gifts for the enrichment of His church.

The words "do not despise prophecies" refer to the various revelatory gifts which uncover stresses, problems, hidden yearnings, or "the secrets of the heart" (see 1 Cor. 14:25).

This uncovering is the first step toward meeting the need. It diagnoses the problem and provides opportunity for divine wisdom to be applied to the source of difficulty. This prophetic gift also has the power to strengthen, encourage and console God's people. Whatever area of need it operates in, it is not to be despised.

Galatians (c. A.D. 48/49)

Gal. 2:1-2. I went up again to Jerusalem . . . by revelation.

The early believers waited on the guidance of the Spirit, and in His timing they received their necessary instructions.

In this verse, Paul probably refers to a revelation that was given to the Church, like that recorded in Acts where the Christians "were worshipping the Lord and fasting" when the Holy Spirit spoke to them (Acts 13:2-3). Or the revelation may have come directly to Paul, or perhaps through some prophet. But whatever the channel, it immediately witnessed in Paul's own heart, and he recognized it as God's word to him.

Gal. 2:9. And when they perceived the grace given to me [they] gave [us] the right hand of fellowship.

The Lord left His signature upon Paul's ministry by allowing signs and wonders to be performed among the Gentiles (Acts 15:12). The word "grace" in this passage contains the thought of "grace-gifts," for an aspect of God's grace was being demonstrated in this supernatural way (Acts 4:33; 11:23).

Gal. 3:2-4. Did you receive the Spirit by works of the law, or by hearing with faith? . . . Did you experience so many things in vain?

Paul took for granted the conscious experience of receiv-

ing the Spirit (see NEB). But he was a realist. Just because
the Spirit had met them earlier in an enriching way in response to their faith, and obviously touched them with His
power, it did not mean Satan would leave them alone, or
that they could not help but continue to walk by faith and
enjoy the Lord. Whatever rich experiences we have had of
salvation and blessing, there are no spiritual heights from
which we cannot fall if we slide into habits of carelessness
and compromise. We commence the Christian life by faith.
We must continue it by faith. Without faith we cannot please
the Lord (Heb. 11:6). No previous attainments, no miraculous
touch of God's hand can be substituted for trusting Him.
The abundance of His grace is given to stimulate and reward
faith, not to replace it.

Gal. 3:5. Does he who supplies the Spirit to you and works miracles among you do so by works of the law, or by hearing with faith?

The *law of God* could never create a miracle of new
birth, but *grace* could do so as people responded in faith!
The law could reveal sin, but only grace operative by faith
could forgive and transform men. The law had no power
to impart the Spirit's gifts, but grace received in faith and
love could open the way for their continuing supply. The
law bears its testimony that we fall short of God's require-
ments and have a need, but faith in Him allows His free,
undeserved grace to operate in all its breadth and height.
As we hear and trust His Word grace is released to express
itself unobtrusively in the heart, or in outward miracles.

God himself was *continuing* to express His life powerfully
among the various churches throughout the Galatian region
(Gal. 1:2). This is stressed by two present participles (*epi-
choregōn* and *energōn*): there was a "further lavish supplying" or "super-adding" of the Spirit to those who had earlier
received the Spirit (see v. 3), and in addition, miracles were
continuing to take place among his readers.

It is quite possible that we have in the use of the word *pneuma* (breath, spirit) a primary reference to the breath of inspiration—an anointing of the Spirit (1 Cor. 14:12, 32). "Spirit" would then be spelled with a small "s." The verse could then be understood: "Does He who continues to supply the inspiration and revelation, and who continues to work miracles among you, do so by the works of the law or by hearing with faith?" Yet however we translate the word here, there is little practical difference, for the Holy Spirit is inseparably linked with divine inspiration, and vice versa.

1 Corinthians (A.D. 54/55)

1 Cor. 1:5-7. In every way you were enriched in him with all speech and all knowledge . . . so that you are not lacking in any spiritual gift.

Paul rejoiced that the Corinthians had received God's grace and lacked no grace-gift. "All speech" refers to spiritual gifts which are verbally expressed, such as prophecy, tongues and interpretation, as well as the ministries of Spirit-anointed preaching and teaching. "All knowledge" covers gifts such as words of knowledge and of wisdom and the discerning of spirits, plus understanding gained through study of His Word and His ways. Paul expected the Christians to keep using these gifts until "the revealing of our Lord Jesus Christ."

1 Cor. 2:4-5. My speech and my message were not in plausible words of wisdom, but in demonstration of the Spirit and power, that your faith might not rest in the wisdom of men but in the power of God.

The word translated "demonstration" (*apodeixis*) emphasizes the Spirit's activity and God's obvious acts of power. These were an unquestionable demonstration that He was genuinely using Paul, and they set the seal of authenticity upon his ministry.

1 Cor. 2:12-14. Now we have received not the spirit of the world, but the Spirit which is from God, that we might understand the gifts bestowed on us by God. And we impart this in words not taught by human wisdom but taught by the Spirit, interpreting spiritual truths to those who possess the Spirit. The unspiritual man does not receive the gifts of the Spirit of God, for they are folly to him, and he is not able to understand them because they are spiritually discerned.

The unspiritual man does not receive or appreciate the gifts, truths and accompaniments of the Holy Spirit, for they operate in a realm unknown to him. Yet they are bestowed as a mark of God's favor (*charisthenta*) upon receptive believers. Like salvation, endowments of the Spirit are undeserved. Only when we come in humble obedience, faith and receptivity can we receive them and understand their ministry and purpose.

1 Cor. 12, 13 and 14. (Spiritual gifts are a necessary provision for the church's vitality, but they are to operate with love.)

2 Corinthians (A.D. 55/56)

2 Cor. 3:7-8. Now if the dispensation of death, carved in letters on stone, came with such splendor that the Israelites could not look at Moses' face because of its brightness, fading as this was, will not the dispensation of the Spirit be attended with greater splendor?

The Holy Spirit is the Life-giver and is able to change us increasingly into the Father's image. As our lives are opened to Him, He teaches, transforms, and empowers us with divine resources to demonstrate His reality and splendor.

2 Cor. 6:4-10. As servants of God we commend ourselves in every way: ... by purity, knowledge, forbearance, kindness, the Holy Spirit, genuine love, truthful speech, and the power of God: with the weapons of righteousness for the right hand and for the left; ... as poor, yet making many rich; as having nothing, and yet possessing everything.

By including "the Holy Spirit" in this passage, the Apostle refers to the gifts and graces of the Spirit which cannot be separated from His person (see NEB).[1] By the phrase "the power of God," he refers in part to his own utterances and ministry which were accompanied by signs and wonders (Rom. 15:18-19; Gal. 3:4-5; 1 Cor. 2:3-5; 2 Cor. 10:4; 12:12) and which revealed divine power at work. The gifts, as we saw earlier, impart power to know, to do, and to speak. "The weapons of righteousness for the right hand and for the left" relates to the completeness of the divine equipment. There is nothing needed that is not available (10:4). God had given Paul and his fellow servants the necessary resources for the fight against all forms of unholiness and satanic power.

2 Cor. 8:7. Now as you excel in everything—in faith, in utterance, in knowledge, in all earnestness, and in your love for us—see that you excel in this gracious work also.

The abundance of spiritual gifts mentioned earlier in 1 Corinthians (1:4-7; 12-14) was continuing unabated. Here, "utterance" (*logos*, see 1 Cor. 1:5) and "knowledge," between them, refer to all the revelatory gifts of the Spirit such as prophecy, tongues, interpretation, words of wisdom and of knowledge, and discernment of spirits. In spite of the Corinthian's shortcomings in many aspects of everyday living, faith and love were present to bind all together. Growth was in fact taking place.

2 Cor. 10:4. The weapons of our warfare are not worldly but have divine power to destroy strongholds.

The Christian Church is engaged in a real war against the powers of darkness. Natural abilities are insufficient, and it is therefore essential that we have the weapons of the Spirit. These include gifts as effective divine weapons of warfare against sin, demonic powers and sickness, and which aid in uncovering and dealing with deep-rooted problems. Through them, victory and release can be brought to those who have been held captive and who desire to escape (Luke 4:18-19).

2 Cor. 12:1-4. I will go on to visions and revelations of the Lord. I know a man in Christ who fourteen years ago was caught up to the third heaven —whether in the body or out of the body I do not know, God knows. And I know that this man was caught up into Paradise—whether in the body or out of the body I do not know, God knows—and he heard things that cannot be told, which man may not utter.

Paul refers to some visions and revelations he had received, but he would not elaborate on them, for not every revelation God gives is for publication. Many are for the individual alone. On the other hand, many did have valuable significance for the young church, but were not recorded within the written Word (v. 12; Acts 5:12; 6:8-10; 14:3-4; 21:9; Rom. 15:17-19; 1 Pet. 4:10).

2 Cor. 12:7-9. And to keep me from being too elated by the abundance of revelations, a thorn was given me in the flesh, a messenger of Satan, to harass me, to keep me from being too elated. Three times I besought the Lord about this, that it should leave me; but he said to me, "My grace is sufficient for you, for my power is made perfect in weakness."

I will all the more gladly boast of my weaknesses, that the power of Christ may rest upon me.

While some of the revelations Paul was given were solely for his own upbuilding, others resulted in his ministering publicly in signs, wonders and mighty works among Christians and non-Christians (v. 12; Rom. 15:17-19). But to keep Paul from complacency and smugness through all that God had shown him, he was subject to almost unrelenting persecution from people who were infuriated by his success in making Christ known. This was a "thorn for the flesh" that God permitted for the bursting of any bubble of arrogance within him.

Paul was never far from hostility and persecution, especially from the religious leaders whose position and affluence were threatened by his ministry. But although God allowed Satan's buffeting to continue, He also used it to create dependence and receptivity in Paul, so that His reviving and inspiring grace could continue to be known. Dedicated abandonment to the Father's will will always be costly, for He has many lessons He can teach only through pain and adversity.

One phrase in particular requires more attention. What did Paul mean by "thorn in the flesh" (*skolops tē sarki*), or "thorn for the flesh" as the NEB margin translates and various commentators prefer?

In a detailed treatment of this passage, Professor Tasker first disagrees with the translation "thorn *in* the flesh," pointing out that if Paul had wished to mean this, he could more naturally have inserted the preposition "in" (*en*) before "the flesh," whereas there is no such word in the original.

On the other hand, if the translation "*for* the flesh" is adopted, then it becomes possible, and indeed more natural, to understand "flesh" in its peculiarly Pauline sense of "the lower nature" which still remains active even in the regenerate; and by "thorn" could be meant painful experiences which pierce this nature from without and prevent it from

> becoming aggressive. . . . It must be acknowledged that the
> general impression of Paul that the reader obtains from
> his Epistles . . . is of a man with an exceptionally strong
> constitution and remarkable powers of physical endurance.
> This is not really compatible with the view that he was the
> constant victim of a severe physical ailment. [2]

This understanding is made more likely in the light of
passages such as Num. 33:55, where Moses warns that if
the children of Israel do not expel the evil inhabitants of
the land before them, they will be "as thorns in your sides,
and they shall trouble you."

Philip Hughes quotes Chrysostom's attitude to this thorn,
this messenger of Satan:

> Chrysostom . . . finds the suggestion that Paul's body was
> given over to Satan for the infliction of physical pain quite
> unacceptable, and, taking the term "Satan" in its general He-
> brew sense of "adversary," understands this "messenger of
> Satan" by whom he was buffeted to signify "Alexander the
> coppersmith, the party of Hymeneus and Philetas, and all
> the adversaries of the word, those who contended with him
> and fought against him, those that cast him into prison,
> those that beat him, that led him away to death; for they
> did Satan's business." [3]

Many scriptures strongly support this view that "the thorn
for the flesh, a messenger of Satan," refers to the harassment Paul was forever experiencing at the hands of the
adversary of human souls (Acts 9:23-29; 13:44-50; 14:1-19;
16:16-24, 37; 17:5-9, 13; 18:6, 12-17; 19:23-41; 20:3; 1 Thess.
2:18). Yet even in the midst of such opposition and persecution, God's grace was sufficient.

When he confronted Elymas, the supply of grace was
accompanied by the grace-gifts of discernment of spirits,
the word of knowledge and the working of a miracle (Acts
13:6-12). On another occasion when Paul was forced out of
one locality, God ministered in grace: "But the unbelieving
Jews stirred up the Gentiles and poisoned their minds against

the brethren. So they remained for a long time, speaking boldly for the Lord, who bore witness to the word of his grace, granting signs and wonders to be done by their hands" (Acts 14:2-3). No wonder Jesus said, "My grace is sufficient for you, for my power is made perfect in weakness." In spite of the harassment, the Lord's continuing strength was available, enabling Paul to serve Him in preaching the gospel, teaching the Word, exhorting and in demonstrating mighty gifts of power. Gifts were there, but much more than that, the Lord Jesus himself accompanied him.

Whatever else is said about other texts on the subject of healing, it is clear that *this* passage cannot be used, as it frequently is, in support of sickness sometimes remaining God's will for His people.

2 Cor. 12:12. The signs of a true apostle were performed among you in all patience, with signs and wonders and mighty works.

"The signs of a true apostle" refers primarily to the transformed lives that were obvious in Corinth as a result of Paul's ministry there (see 1 Cor. 9:1-2). "Signs" in the phrase "signs and wonders" emphasize that these expressions of God's power were valuable teaching aids. They had *sign*ificant content, and God was using them as one means of educating men to His reality and character. "Wonders," by their novelty, amaze, capture attention, and make sincere men thoughtful. "Mighty works" demonstrate God's power in unaccustomed yet unmistakable ways. These powerfully confirmed Paul's apostolic calling.

Romans (c. A.D. 58)

Rom. 1:11-12. I long to see you, that I may impart to you some spiritual gift to strengthen you, that is, that we may be mutually encouraged by each other's faith, both yours and mine.

The Church is both strengthened and established (*stēri-*

zō) when it receives gifts. Without these it must remain incomplete, unbalanced and lack strength and maturity in some areas. No church has ever yet received all God's provision, and the Roman church was no exception.

Paul desired that the enrichment they would receive would flow back in blessing to himself, for then their love and Body-ministry would refresh his own spirit. Spiritual "fathers," and even apostles, benefit from the encouragement and ministry that new Christians bring.

> **Rom. 8:9. You are not in the flesh, you are in the Spirit, if the Spirit of God really dwells in you. Any one who does not have the Spirit of Christ does not belong to him.**

James Dunn has aptly written that

The thing which determines whether a man is a Christian is not his profession of faith in Christ but the presence of the Spirit. "If anyone does not have the Spirit," says Paul, "he is no Christian"; "*Only those* who are led by the Spirit of God are sons of God" (v. 14). He does not say, If you are Christ's you have the Spirit, or, If you are sons you have the Spirit, far less, If you have believed all the right things and/or have been baptized (and so are a Christian) you have the Spirit. In the earliest days of Christianity possession of the Spirit was a fact of *immediate* perception, not a logical conclusion to be drawn from the performance of an ecclesiastical rite. [4]

> **Rom. 8:26-27. Likewise the Spirit helps us in our weakness; for we do not know how to pray as we ought, but the Spirit himself intercedes for us with sighs too deep for words. And he who searches the hearts of men knows what is the mind of the Spirit, because the Spirit intercedes for the saints according to the will of God.**

We, like the Apostle, are greatly limited in knowing how

to pray with understanding, for our human intellect and knowledge are severely restricted. Often we know neither what prayer to offer, nor how to offer it. At these times, the Holy Spirit can anoint and inspire us so that the normal limits of understanding or inclination are completely surpassed. Deep thoughts and longings which are inexpressible in ordinary speech well up from our beings, and the Spirit who searches the heart takes them and presents them to God by a means of communication which He himself inspires. In this, the prayer is neither from the Spirit alone, nor the individual alone, but with the co-operation of both. At these times God the Spirit prays with yearnings and sighs from deep within us, making us aware of His very heartbeat, emotions, desires, viewpoint.

This portion of scripture closely parallels 1 Corinthians 12-14, where Paul discusses praying to God in the Spirit with tongues. Paul could not make the statements he did in 1 Corinthians—such as "one who speaks in a tongue speaks not to men but to God; for no one understands him, but he utters mysteries in the spirit" (see 1 Cor. 14:2, 14-15)— yet omit the thought of praying in tongues here in Romans 8, for this would exclude one of the deepest expressions of Spirit-aided prayer. No other kind of prayer corresponds more exactly with praying with the Spirit.

There is another kind of Spirit-guided prayer that also involves gifts of the Spirit (see comments on Eph. 6:18 in this chapter), but it is something different from that which Paul describes in these verses.

Rom. 10:12. The same Lord is Lord of all and bestows his riches upon all who call upon him.

God's riches are vast and of infinite variety, and include the gifts of the Spirit with all their enriching qualities. He delights to give out of this abundance to all who will accept His ministry.

**Rom. 12:3-8. For by the grace given to me I bid
every one among you not to think of himself more
highly than he ought to think, but to think with sober
judgment, each according to the measure of faith
which God has assigned him. For as in one body we
have many members, and all the members do not
have the same function, so we, though many, are one
body in Christ, and individually members one of another. Having gifts that differ according to the grace
given to us, let us use them: if prophecy, in propor-
tion to our faith; if service, in our serving; he who
teaches, in his teaching; he who exhorts, in his exhortation; he who contributes, in liberality; he who
gives aid, with zeal; he who does acts of mercy,
with cheerfulness.**

The "grace" given to Paul in verse 3 refers to the spiritual gift of apostleship (see Rom. 1:5; Eph. 4:7-11) which
he is responsible for using. Likewise each member is to
exercise his own respective grace or spiritual gift for the
good of all.

The grace-gifts mentioned (*charismata*) embrace both the
miraculous and the more natural without distinction. Prophecy, serving, teaching, exhortation, liberality, giving aid,
and acts of mercy are all gifts. No Christian is limited to
ministering just one of these, for he may be used in all
or most of them. For example, exhorting, the liberal giving
of time, money or both as God gives opportunity, the doing
of acts of mercy, or the receiving of an anointing to prophesy,
are ministries in which *all* can participate at His direction.
"Prophecy" here is used in its broader sense to include
any of the revelatory gifts such as words of wisdom and
of knowledge, discernment of spirits, or a direct prophetic
message. (See comments on 1 Cor. 12:10.) But however we
serve, we must do so in the power and love of God, so that
more than surface needs are met.

Rom. 12:11. Be aglow with the Spirit.

This verse can also be rendered, "Be fervent (or aglow) in spirit," but as this is only possible when the human spirit is activated and inspired by the holy Breath of God himself, there is little practical difference in either translation.

It is our responsibility to see that the fire is kept burning upon the altar continuously (see Lev. 6:13). Once the fire has started, it must be maintained and fed with the oil of the Spirit. Communion with the Lord, meditation upon His Word and obedience to it will keep us open to the repeated infilling of the Spirit and the revelation which He brings. When Moses ascended Mount Sinai, he spent six days being prepared before hearing the Lord's voice, but when he finally came down, "the skin of his face shone because he had been talking with God," and "the Israelites could not look at Moses' face because of its brightness" (Ex. 24:15-18; 34:29; 2 Cor. 3:7).

By far the greatest and most regular way God guides is by opening the Scriptures. In this way He brings light and life to our spirit as the two found on their way to Emmaus: "Did not our hearts burn within us while he talked to us on the road, while he opened to us the scriptures?" (Luke 24:32).

Frequently our problem is not that we need further revelation of God's will, but that we do not take seriously the scriptures which already clearly reveal it. If we ignore scriptural truth, we will have no lasting benefits from any additional revelation.

Rom. 14:17. For the kingdom of God does not mean food and drink but righteousness and peace and joy in the Holy Spirit.

Within Scripture, the kingdom of God is associated with the supernatural realm where the living God reigns. By the ministry of inspired teaching, healing and deliverance begun by Jesus and continued through the Church, evil powers were being broken, and men and women were surrendering themselves to His kingly reign (Matt. 4:23-24). After a blind and dumb demoniac had been brought to Jesus and both healed and delivered, Jesus said, "If it is by the Spirit of God that I cast out demons, then the kingdom of God has come upon you" (Matt. 12:22-28; see also 10:7-8; 1 Cor. 4:20). Here He linked the thought of the kingdom with supernatural liberation from Satan's grip, and the compulsion to unrighteous and useless living. When God reigns, He brings righteousness, peace and joy, for the Spirit opposes evil in all its forms (1 Thess. 1:6; Acts 2:42-47).

Rom. 15:18-19. For I will not venture to speak of anything except what Christ has wrought through me to win obedience from the Gentiles, by word and deed, by the power of signs and wonders, by the power of the Holy Spirit, so that from Jerusalem and as far round as Illyricum I have fully preached the gospel of Christ.

During Paul's ministry, attention was gained and obedience won not only by his spoken words and godly life. God added to these His divine signature by giving accompanying miracles and signs. In this way the Lord himself supplied evidence of His approval and power and authenticated Paul's service. The living God (1 Tim. 4:10) could not be communicated solely by correct exegetical or theological study. For his part, the Apostle is not ashamed of seeking to win Gentiles through gifts of the Spirit released in the performing of signs and wonders. For Paul, "fully preaching the gospel of Christ" included much more than words of truth, for preaching and gifts were interwoven inseparably. Both proclaimed with equal clarity the love and intervention of a Father who was concerned about His children's needs, and perfectly able to meet them. Faith and works went together.

Colossians (A.D. 60/61)

Col. 1:9-12. We have not ceased to pray for you, asking that you may be filled with the knowledge of his will in all spiritual wisdom and understanding, to lead a life worthy of the Lord, fully pleasing to him, bearing fruit in every good work and increasing in the knowledge of God. May you be strengthened with all power, according to his glorious might, for all endurance and patience with joy, giving thanks to the Father, who has qualified us to share in the inheritance of the saints in light.

Because the gifts of the Spirit were operating within the universal church (1 Cor. 12:28), this prayer would find a partial answer as God ministered through revelatory gifts to give understanding and wisdom supernaturally. The Apostle wanted his readers "to lead a life worthy of the Lord" in character, authority and power—a life that pleased Him and was fruitful, practical and informed. Knowledge of God was to be gained by responding to apostolic teaching and example, through meditation on scripture, and by direct revelation.

We all need supernatural power and the spiritual gifts operating within each local fellowship before we can enter fully into our Christian inheritance.

Col. 3:16. Let the word of Christ dwell in [or among] you richly.

Much of the New Testament had yet to be written, collated and circulated when Paul penned these words. The Colossians therefore knew that *the word (logos) of Christ* which was to dwell in its rich fullness among them included the continuing Spirit-given endowments which passed the tests of revelation, testified to Jesus, and glorified Him. As they gathered in their assemblies, each worshipper was responsible for being sensitive to the Lord, so that His words to the congregation—through the Old Testament, authoritative epistles, and gifts of the Spirit—might be received and shared in all their richness and abundance.

> **. . . as you teach and admonish one another in all wisdom, and as you sing psalms and hymns and spiritual songs with thankfulness in your hearts to God.**

Teaching from the Scriptures will always be an essential part of worship, for His Word is a lamp to our feet and a light to our path (Ps. 119: 103-107). It bears witness to Him (John 5:39) and is profitable in many ways (2 Tim. 3:16-17). But God teaches, not only from the Scriptures, but also when He gives specific words of wisdom and other revelatory gifts for particular situations.

A comparison of this passage with its parallel in Eph. 5:18-19, shows that teaching, singing and the enjoyment of the Lord are associated with the Spirit's fullness and with the word of Christ. These are closely connected in the New Testament because only when filled with the Spirit is it possible for the Lord's words to dwell richly among us. (For "spiritual songs," see Eph. 5:17-19.)

> **Col. 4:17. See that you fulfil the ministry which you have received in the Lord.**

The Lord has given every Christian a ministry (*diakonia*) suited to his own relationship to Him and his stage of spiritual development (1 Cor. 12:4-11; 1 Pet. 4:10-11; 2 Tim. 4:5). No commission, however humble, should be neglected or despised in favor of reaching out for that which is more prominent or spectacular, for every function is necessary and important to the Lord. He appreciates what may seem the insignificant ministry of a cup of water when it is given in His name.

On the other hand, we are not to be puffed up or smug, nor think more highly of ourselves and our service than we ought. Both Saul and Uzziah are sad examples of those who sought to take upon themselves a ministry to which they were not called, for they moved into the area of another's God-given ministry and out of the area and protection of their own, with disastrous results (1 Sam. 13:8-14; 2 Chron. 26:16-17). The Lord wants us to fulfill *our* own ministry, without trying in pride or self-will to override its boundaries or shirk its demands.

Ephesians (c. A.D. 61/62)

Before examining specific passages in the Ephesian letter, it is beneficial to draw together what we know of the background to the operation of the gifts within Ephesus.

That all the gifts of the Spirit in Corinth also operated in Ephesus is clear from the following: (1) Tongues and prophecy were experienced by Ephesian Christians (Acts 19:1-7). (2) While Paul was at Ephesus (from where he wrote 1 Cor.), he mentioned the grace-gifts which the Spirit gives to believers. He then detailed some of those gifts, and testified that at the time of writing he spoke in tongues more than they did. He was not ashamed of it, thanked God for it, and commended it to all his readers. From Ephesus he spoke of tongues as prayer and taught that it glorified God and was edifying to the believer. He also spoke of the greater instructional value of prophecy in congregational worship. While he was there he mentioned that the gifts in Corinth were to be rightly permitted in open, corporate worship (1 Cor. 14:26-32). (3) While in Ephesus, Paul wrote that the church at Corinth was meant to exercise *all* the organs of the Body for its correct function. He expected the Body in Corinth to need hands and feet, eyes, ears and nose—and he knew the Body of Christ *in Ephesus* (or in any other place) was incomplete without such essential organs. If this was not so, he would be contradicting all he had written in 1 Corinthians 12. (4) Paul stated that during his three-year

Ephesian ministry he "did not shrink from declaring to them anything that was profitable," and that he declared "the whole counsel of God" (see Acts 20:20-31). This must therefore have included teaching on the Spirit's gifts which profit the individual and the Body (e.g., 1 Cor. 12:7).

And so when Paul teaches the Corinthians about the gifts and his own experience of them, he expresses his thoughts while living in Ephesus. He would not correct a distant congregation's problem of ignorance about spiritual gifts (1 Cor. 12:1) without also informing the church where he was currently fellowshipping of the same truths.

Eph. 1:3, 7-8. Blessed be the God and Father of our Lord Jesus Christ, who has blessed us in Christ with every spiritual blessing in the heavenly places. . . . In him we have redemption through his blood, the forgiveness of our trespasses, according to the riches of his grace which he lavished upon us.

God is infinitely gracious and He delights to pour out upon us a continuous flow of undeserved material and spiritual blessings. The reference to being blessed with "every spiritual blessing" is far wider than the spiritual gifts of 1 Corinthians 12-14, but they represent some of God's abundance, and cannot be excluded from the reference here. They must be given their rightful place among other equally important "riches of his grace." [5]

God's grace is rich beyond all our understanding. He "richly furnishes us with everything to enjoy" (1 Tim. 6:17). "We have our hope set on the living God" (1 Tim. 4:10)—and, we might add, "the giving God" as well (e.g., Ps. 36:8-9; Matt. 16:19; Luke 11:13; John 10:28; Acts 17:25; Rom. 8:32; 2 Cor. 9:15; Eph. 4:11; Phil. 4:19; James 1:5). How much we should worship Him!

Eph. 1:13-14. In him you also, who have heard the word of truth, the gospel of your salvation, and have believed in him, were sealed with the promised Holy Spirit, which is the guarantee of our inheritance. . . .

Within scripture, a seal implies an external mark or impression (e.g., Jer. 32:11-14; Ezek. 9:4; Matt. 27:66).[7] But what was the exact nature of this "seal of the Spirit" that Paul mentions three times? (See also 2 Cor. 1:22 and Eph. 4:30.)

Clearly it refers to the charismatic outpouring of the Spirit which the Lord's followers experienced in an obvious way (Acts 2:4; 8:14-21; 10:44-48; 11:16-17; 19:1-7; Rom. 8:9). When the Ephesian disciples of Acts 19 heard these words from Paul's letter, they would have immediately recalled that memorable day when they had been instructed by Paul, baptized, and then received the Spirit with the customary grace-gifts as Paul laid his hands upon each of them in turn. Now, however, not only these twelve but all the Ephesian Christians had received this obvious seal.

Under the Old Covenant, circumcision was the seal (Rom. 4:11): under the New, the sovereign outpouring of the Spirit evidenced by charismatic gifts (but not dissociated from baptism) became the recognizable seal of God's ownership and authentication. In this way God stamped the obedient believer as His property and put His trademark upon him.

Many further evidences of the Spirit's presence must also appear in the Christian's life. Though the fruit of the Spirit (Gal. 5:22-23) is not harvested the moment the seed is sown, growth must begin and be encouraged to mature. Christian principles taught by our Lord in the Sermon on the Mount need to be outworked in the life (Matt. 5-7), and moral transformation must take place (1 Cor. 6:9-11; 1 Thess. 1:9; 2

Thess. 2:13). The "*seal* of the Spirit" did not, however, refer to these essential aspects, but to the previous event when God's acceptance of them was first acknowledged by the Spirit's evident outpouring.

> **Eph. 1:17-19. [Paul prays] that the God of our Lord Jesus Christ, the Father of glory, may give you a spirit of wisdom and of revelation in the knowledge of him, having the eyes of your hearts enlightened, that you may know what is the hope to which he has called you, what are the riches of his glorious inheritance in the saints, and what is the immeasurable greatness of his power in us who believe.**

Here *pneuma* without the definite article (in the phrase "a spirit of wisdom and of revelation") refers to some special expression or bestowal of the Holy Spirit, when the incoming Wind of God pervades our spirits with His living breath, giving a spiritual capacity and capability not otherwise known (see 1 Cor. 14:12, 32).

Paul wanted his readers to experience God's limitless blessings which would affect character, calling, inheritance, and bring to fruition God's full purpose for His children. He prays for a new realization of His power, using the resurrection from the dead as the standard of what He can do!

> **Eph. 2:6-7. God . . . raised us up with him, and made us sit with him in the heavenly places in Christ Jesus, that in the coming ages he might show the immeasurable riches of his grace in kindness toward us in Christ Jesus.**

The Lord Jesus is seated upon the throne of the universe, the symbol of supreme authority, and the believer is seated in the same exalted position with Him—sharing His throne!

This means that His very own authority is given us over sin and the evil power of darkness rampant in the world (see 1:19-22)! Implied in these verses is the delegated authority and power available to us in Christ to discern and deal with principalities and powers and reverse or negate the conditions which they have produced.

Eph. 4:7. But grace was given to each of us.

"Grace" here alludes to the gifts described in Rom. 12:3-8 and 1 Cor. 12:4-11. To enable Christians to serve God adequately, everyone in the Body of Christ has been endowed with some gift-by-grace (*charisma*). And it is the ascended Lord who bestows these gifts by first sending His supreme gift of the Holy Spirit (John 7:39; 20:22; Acts 2:33).

Eph. 4:8-13. When [Christ] ascended . . . he gave gifts to men. . . . And his gifts were that some should be apostles, some prophets, some evangelists, some pastors and teachers, for the equipment of the saints, for the work of ministry, for building up the body of Christ, until we all attain to the unity of the faith, and of the knowledge of the Son of God, to mature manhood, to the measure of the stature of the fullness of Christ.

The difference between the list of gifts (*domata*) here and that in 1 Cor. 12:8-10 is that there gifts are the supernatural endowment of the Holy Spirit to the individual, while the gifts listed here represent *ministries* given by Jesus to the Church. In the former, the natural abilities of the Spirit —which we consider supernatural—are *given to people* for a specific task, whereas *here the gifts are people*, with supernatural equipment for their office. They are Christians whom Jesus appoints and guides "to equip God's people for work in his service, to the building up of the body of Christ"

(NEB). Apostles, prophets, evangelists, pastors and teachers have a God-appointed responsibility to bring all the Lord's people to spiritual fitness so that they in turn can live effectively and use the grace-gifts they each receive (see 1 Cor. 12:31; 14:1). In other words, Jesus appointed leadership ministries and gave them divine equipment for their task to enable them to serve their fellow Christians effectively, that they in turn could minister effectively to the Lord, each other and the world.

Some should be apostles. Scripture uses the title "apostle" both in a narrow and a broader sense. The Twelve were the first apostles, then Paul, but afterwards the title was extended to include others like Barnabas, James the Lord's brother, Andronicus and Junias, Silvanus (Silas), and Timothy (Acts 14:4, 14; 1 Cor. 9:5-6; Gal. 1:19; 2:9; Rom. 16:7; 1 Thess. 2:6 with 1:1), and others unknown to us by name (1 Cor. 15:7). An essential qualification of an apostle was to have seen the risen Lord during the historic occasions of the first Easter, or to have witnessed His ascended glory through a verifiable vision coupled with a definite commissioning by the Lord (see Acts 9:3-16; 1 Cor. 9:1-2). The "signs of an apostle" were also verifiable in the spiritual fruit produced, and in the "signs and wonders and mighty works" that accompanied his ministry (2 Cor. 12:12). God appointed apostles to plant churches (Eph. 2:20), appoint elders, guard the original faith and practice that the Lord had given (2 Tim. 2:2), and build up the Body of Christ.

It is the writer's conviction that the ministry of apostleship continues today, and that the Church should pray that God will raise up more apostles for ministry to His Body, but it is outside the scope of this study to examine such a view.

Some prophets. As we saw earlier, the prophet speaks from the impulse of an immediate revelation (1 Cor. 14:30). While every believer can manifest the Spirit in prophecy when under the necessary anointing of the Spirit, not all are called to *a ministry* of prophecy, that is, to be designated "prophets" (1 Cor. 12:29; 14:5, 31). The prophetic *office* was much more limited, for comparatively few were called to this responsible and special ministry of waiting upon the Lord and seeking His mind for the church. Because of this special call of God and the greater responsibility of ministry, the prophet will be recognized as someone of greater faith (Rom. 12:6) and with a greater depth of revelation in his ministry. Prediction is more likely, as are other gifts of power (Acts 11:28; 21:10-11).

Some evangelists. The word means "one who proclaims the good news"—one who declares the message of God's grace.

All Christians have the responsibility and privilege of being witnesses to Christ and proclaiming the gospel, yet some have this as a special function. Timothy is to "do the work of an evangelist" (2 Tim. 4:5), though no details are added as to what would be involved. Philip is the only other evangelist mentioned within the New Testament (Acts 21:8), so the record of his work is the only inspired account that shows us the evangelist's methods and the accompaniments of his ministry (Acts 8:4-40). Whereas signs, wonders and mighty deeds accompanied true apostles, Acts demonstrates that the Spirit-filled evangelist's ministry (Acts 6:3-6) was marked by preaching the word, by revelation (Acts 8:26, 29), and the performing of mighty works of deliverance and healing: "Philip went down to a city of Samaria, and proclaimed to them the Christ. And the multitudes with one accord gave heed to what was said by Philip, when they heard him and saw the signs which he did. For unclean spirits came out of many who were possessed, crying with a loud voice, and many who were paralyzed or lame were healed" (Acts 8:5-7). Signs, wonders and spoken words demonstrated God's reality and love and convinced many of the Lord's claim on their lives.

Some pastors and teachers. A pastor, that is, a shepherd, is also referred to as an overseer or an elder (see note on 1 Cor. 12:28). His duty was to shepherd the flock of God (1 Pet. 5:1-4; Acts 20:28), that is, to feed, protect and care for it. Every overseer or elder must be competent to teach the essentials of the faith (1 Tim. 3:2). Yet some possess this gift to a far greater degree. Eldership allows for variations of ministry so that while all elders rule or oversee the church, some are especially responsible for laboring in preaching and teaching (1 Tim. 5:17). Sometimes such a ministry is even more prominent and the gift is recognized as a teacher (1 Cor. 12:28).

A "teacher" who is not one in name only is an extremely important gift. He depends upon the Spirit's direction and anointing as he waits on the Lord for his message (John 7:16; 2 Tim. 2:15; 1 Cor. 2:14; 11:23). Through his logical messages from the Word he appeals to the spiritual, intellectual and logical faculties of his congregation, so that they may intelligently present themselves to God to become workmen who rightly handle the word of truth for themselves.

The teacher assists Christians to love the Lord their God with all their minds as well as with heart, soul and strength (Mark 12:30), and prepares them for making their defense before any who call them to account for the hope within them (1 Pet. 3:15). Through his ministry, living scriptural truth is able to correct any false pattern of thought and action (Eph. 4:23).

Under God's anointing the teaching ministry has immense power to bring renewal and life. Its importance cannot be over-estimated. Yet it can easily grow lax, for teaching can be brought from the Bible even if the Spirit's direction and anointing has lifted. Then, instead of imparting life and liberty from the Spirit, the teacher begins to minister law and death through a basically human message (2 Cor. 3:6). It is then comparatively easy for him to cause division or stagnation within the church, for he controls the direction of the teaching given, and through ignorance, tradition or deception he can deride, dismiss or minimize that which he does not personally believe or experience. He has a major responsibility to be receptive to the Spirit's revelation while recognizing that his knowledge, like all others, is imperfect (1 Cor. 13:9), and that because of his position he will be judged by God with greater strictness (James 3:1).

All who make up the Church of Jesus Christ—whether they are apostles, prophets, evangelists, pastors, teachers, administrators, or any others—are earnestly to desire spiritual gifts. They who are called the gift of Christ are to desire the Spirit's gifts for the fulfillment of their ministry, as none are sufficient without His equipment and enabling.

> **Eph. 5:18-19. Do not get drunk with wine, for that is debauchery; but be filled with the Spirit, addressing one another in psalms and hymns and spiritual songs, singing and making melody to the Lord with all your heart, always and for everything giving thanks in the name of our Lord Jesus Christ to God the Father.**

After the 120 were filled with the Spirit and spoke in tongues at Pentecost, some who lacked insight derided the obvious joy within the Christians and dismissed them as drunk. But there was a better explanation! So when Paul wrote to the Ephesians he showed the complete contrast between the debasing of drunkenness and the renewing life of the Spirit. In giving the command to be filled, he used a particular form of the verb (present imperative passive) which can be brought out by translating: "Let the Spirit fill you repeatedly, continuously."

We all need to lead a life which is constantly open to the Lord so that the repeated filling with the Spirit, as experienced in the New Testament (e.g., Acts 2:4; 4:8, 31; 9:17-18; 13:9-11), becomes continuous reality for us! To be filled with the Spirit means to be filled with the Spirit's inspiration, that is, filled with the inspiring breath of God, and enabled to worship, speak, know, or act with divine and supernatural power. Recalling that the word *pneuma* is without the definite article here, we can paraphrase the Greek (*plērousthe en pneumati*), "Let the transforming, inspiring, enabling Breath of God fill you repeatedly." God intends that individually and collectively we be constantly open to the total ministry of His Spirit.

"Addressing one another" corresponds to the fuller phrase "teach and admonish one another" in Col. 3:16. Christians are to address one another "in psalms and hymns and spiritual songs." "Spiritual songs" or "songs which the Spirit inspires" refers to singing with the Spirit, that is, in tongues (see 1 Cor. 14:15). In the free-flowing church worship there would be the singing of regular hymns such as found in the Psalms and other scripture passages, plus unrehearsed melodies both in the language of the congregation and in tongues as the Spirit directs (see Col. 3:16).

Eph. 6:15. The equipment of the gospel of peace.

We are all engaged in a real war against principalities and powers. But for such a battle, the Father offers divine equipment to all who want to go forward with God. When Paul wrote to the Roman Christians, he related how he himself was provided with armaments for winning obedience from the Gentiles, "by word and deed, by the power of signs and wonders, by the power of the Holy Spirit" (Rom. 15:18-19). In addition to Paul's qualities of character there was this outward ministry of miracles and signs. By what he did, by what he said and by what he was, he brought the gospel of peace to the troubled and sin-laden.

Today the Church requires the same equipment to meet the same needs.

Eph. 6:17. And take . . . the sword of the Spirit, which is the word of God.

For fighting spiritual battles and ministering to other

members of the Body of Christ or those in the world, we need "the sword of the Spirit, which is the word of God" (*rhēma Theou*). The New English Bible captures the Apostle's thought: "For sword, take that which the Spirit gives you—the words that come from God." Here Paul alludes to all the words God gives and which are perfectly applicable to the particular situation—for example, words from scripture which come to life by the Spirit's illumination, as well as the revelatory gifts of the Spirit such as prophecy and words of wisdom or of knowledge. The power to discern and cast out evil spirits is another continuing part of the equipment to bring peace and life.

These gifts become the Spirit's sword to use in specific instances in the attack against Satan's evil realm, following the example of Jesus who likewise fought and used "every word [*rhēma*] that proceeds from the mouth of God" (Matt. 4:4).

Eph. 6:18. Pray at all times in the Spirit, with all [kinds of] prayer and supplication.

"Praying in the Spirit" here and in Jude 20[8] refers to the co-operative flow in prayer of the Holy Spirit with the believer. It refers to praying under inspiration (*pneuma*). The Spirit inspires, guides, energizes and prompts its expression. Praying with the Spirit implies that we do not pray for what *we* want but for that which God purposes and plans. Praying in tongues is one form of praying with the Spirit. It by-passes the mind's natural limitations and gives free rein to the Spirit's inspiration.

Besides tongues, there is another kind of praying with the Spirit. For example, God can supernaturally reveal someone's need by a direct word of knowledge, and show us the mind of the Spirit as to what and how to pray in English, so that we know we are praying in the will of God. That too involves gifts of the Spirit and is Spirit-guided prayer.

Philippians (c. A.D. 61/62)

Phil. 3:3. We . . . worship by the Spirit of God [9] and glory in Christ Jesus, and put no confidence in the flesh.

Acceptable worship is Spirit-guided worship (see 1 Cor. 14:15-16). What ultimately matters is that our worship and service are open to the Spirit's renewing, energizing and inspiring ministry. Worship brought in response to His prompting will always lead to an exulting in Christ Jesus and a lack of confidence in mere human attainment or worth.

Phil. 3:17 and 4:9. Brethren, join in imitating me. . . . What you have learned and received and heard and seen in me, do. . . .

Paul was humbly grateful that God had graciously enriched him with gifts and graces. And because he had learned and received so much, he was able to teach God's will, and minister in power and authority among men. Paul wanted his readers to follow his example. They were to be as receptive to God's truth and grace as he was.

James (A.D. 58-62) [10]

James 1:17. Every good endowment and every perfect gift is from above, coming down from the Father of lights with whom there is no variation or shadow due to change.

James 4:5-6. Do you suppose it is in vain that the scripture says, "He yearns jealously over the spirit [or Spirit] which He has made to dwell in us"? But he gives more grace. . . . "God opposes the proud, but gives grace to the humble."

God is unchanging, and His Father-heart always delights to demonstrate His grace and love by lavishing His endowments upon His children. All His varying gifts express His graciousness, while those specifically called the "gifts of the Spirit" emphasize His supernatural nature. It is the humble who will receive the greatest and most edifying outpourings of His grace. From them will come the purest manifestations, for their motives do not hinder the divine flow of life.

James 5:13-16. Is any one among you suffering? Let him pray. . . . Is any among you sick? Let him call for the elders of the church, and let them pray over him, anointing him with oil in the name of the Lord; and the prayer of faith will save the sick man, and the Lord will raise him up; and if he has committed sins, he will be forgiven. Therefore confess your sins to one another, and pray for one another, that you may be healed.

James shows that the doorway into healing is wide open, provided we follow His instructions. God wants us to be whole in spirit and in body, but there can be an important connection between spiritual and physical healing. It is no use praying for physical healing if there is spiritual ill-health due to sin. The spiritual block must first be removed before we can claim God's power for physical renewal.

1 Timothy (c. A.D. 63)

1 Tim. 4:1. The Spirit expressly says . . .

There was nothing vague or dubious about the way the Spirit was speaking to Paul. Whether the revelation came directly to him or through another, the message was clear-cut and distinct, and obviously imparted by the Spirit.

1 Tim. 4:13-14. Till I come, attend to the public reading of scripture, to preaching, to teaching. Do not neglect the gift you have, which was given you by prophetic utterance when the elders laid their hands upon you.

The Lord had previously revealed Timothy's calling and area of ministry (see also 2 Tim. 1:6-7), and Paul now refers back to these same prophecies and shows they retained their teaching value even many years later.

Titus (c. A.D. 63)

Titus 3:4-6. God our Savior . . . saved us . . . in virtue of his own mercy, by the washing of regeneration and renewal in the Holy Spirit, which he poured out upon us richly through Jesus Christ our Savior.

When we place these words side by side with other references, we see how very pentecostal they are.

The Holy Spirit was *"poured out"* (Joel 2:28; Acts 2:17-18, 33, 10:45)—*"upon us"* (Luke 24:49; Acts 2:17-18; 8:16; 10:44; 11:15; 19:6)—*"richly"* (John 7:38-39; Acts 2:11, 32-33; 8:17-19; 10:46; 11:15-16)—*"through Jesus Christ"* (Mark 1:8; John 1:33; Acts 2:33). Paul recalls the rich, conscious reception of the Spirit that came upon all believers, and upon himself and Titus specifically. Neither of them had been present at Pentecost, but like those who were Christians before them, each had experienced the fullness of the pentecostal deluge for themselves and the rich ˙supply of the Spirit which resulted from this outpouring (see Joel 2:28-29). This dynamic encounter is variously described in the New Testament, and provides the essential foundation for full ministry in the Holy Spirit.

2 Timothy (c. A.D. 66)

2 Tim. 1:6-7. I remind you to rekindle the gift of God that is within you through the laying on of my hands; for God did not give us a spirit of timidity but a spirit of power and love and self-control.

Paul reminded Timothy to stir into a living flame (or "keep in full flame") the special gift of ministry God had given him through the Apostle (see 1 Tim. 1:18; 4:14). It is perilously easy to allow reticence, timidity or fear to restrain true spiritual gifts, and to withhold a ministry. But God wants men to count on the power, love and self-control available in Him.

2 Tim. 2:2. What you have heard from me before many witnesses entrust to faithful men who will be able to teach others also.

By its nature this verse is closely connected with the lives of Paul and Timothy who were such devoted companions (2 Tim. 1:13-14; 3:10). Timothy had close associations with the Apostle both in Corinth (2 Cor. 1:19; Rom. 16:21) and Ephesus (1 Cor. 4:17; 1 Tim. 1:3), and knew what Paul taught "everywhere in every church" (1 Cor. 4:17). So Paul was confident that Timothy could teach the same truths which he himself declared wherever he went. There was nothing given to one particular congregation that was to be withheld from another. If it was for one, it was for all. It is clear from Paul's emphasis on the value of the Spirit's gifts and their functioning with love that both gifts and love would be included among the subjects "for teaching others also." You cannot have love without expression and you cannot have edifying expression without love. Timothy's congregation, no less than the Corinthians, was to be informed of the need of both (see 1 Cor. 12:1).

2 Tim. 3:16-17. All scripture is inspired by God and profitable for teaching, for reproof, for correction, and for training in righteousness, that the man of God may be complete, equipped for every good work.

The Word of God owes its origin and content to the divine Breath, the Spirit of God. It was inspired—literally, "God-breathed" (*Theopneustos*)—as the grace-gifts operated through a wide variety of writers. When Paul penned these words the writing of the Scriptures had not been finished, whereas they are now complete. Inspired and revealed directly by the Spirit, the Bible remains the ultimate standard of truth by which all preaching, teaching, revelation and practice must be subservient and judged. Subsequent revelations may parallel, illustrate, amplify or personalize it, but God's voice through continuing revelation and preaching will always harmonize with that already revealed. They will always further the honor and glory of the Lord Jesus Christ and reveal His character, power and supreme authority.

1 Peter (c. A.D. 63/64)

1 Pet. 1:13. Set your hope fully upon the grace that is coming to you at the revelation of Jesus Christ.

The verse can be more precisely translated: "Set your hope fully upon the grace that is being brought to you in (*en*) the revealing (or revelation) of Jesus Christ." God's grace had been revealed at the first advent (Titus 2:11) and would be further seen at His final return in glory (1 Pet. 1:7; 4:13), but between the advents, grace was being expressed through the same Spirit who had filled Jesus. Jesus was still reaching out His hand to heal and perform further signs and wonders (see Acts 4:29-31). There would still be the revelation of His character, power and authority in specific situations among new generations of men.

1 Pet. 4:10-11. As each has received a gift, employ it for one another, as good stewards of God's varied grace: whoever speaks, as one who utters oracles of God; whoever renders service, as one who renders it by the strength which God supplies; in order that in everything God may be glorified through Jesus Christ.

Peter could assume that every Christian in a wide geographical area (Pontus, Galatia, Cappadocia, Asia and Bithynia) had received a grace-gift (*charisma*) from the Lord. These were given to enrich others and glorify Jesus Christ. Each believer should remember that he was a steward of what God had placed in his hands, and one day he must give account (see Matt. 25:24-30; Luke 12:42-48; 16:1-8; 1 Cor. 4:1-2).

Spiritual gifts vary widely from the miraculous to the more regular (Rom. 12:3-8; 1 Cor. 1:7; 7:7; 12-14; 1 Tim. 4:14; Eph. 4:11-12). and Peter himself exercised a very large number of both kinds. Tongues, healings, prophecy, working of miracles, words of wisdom and of knowledge, discernment of spirits and deliverance, plus unspecified signs and wonders were among the distinctly supernatural gifts manifested in his own life. Probably there were others as well. Peter now classifies them all into gifts involving the utterance of divine truth, and gifts of "rendering service."

Each one who speaks should be as one who utters "oracles of God"—a term relating to the inspired writings of the Old Testament (see Acts 7:38; Rom. 3:2). That is, he was to be receptive to any form of direct revelation so that when he spoke to an individual or to the congregation, he presented not human insights but God's own words and wisdom. And as he ministered he was to recognize his sacred responsibility, so that God would be glorified by the manner and content of the utterance.

Every one of God's gifts are practical, but there are many that are demonstrated in caring, loving, comforting and providing hospitality for others. Yet whatever the area of ministry, we should exercise all for God's glory.

It is clear that those used in direct revelation must also serve in other practical ways. Equally, those who give practical help need not be restricted solely to one area of spiritual gift, for everyone can be used in at least one of the power gifts of 1 Cor. 12:8-10. For example, Philip and Stephen who were appointed to "serve tables" also exercised an evangelistic gift with signs accompanying, or taught and "did great wonders and signs" (Acts 6:1-8; 8:5-8).

Jude (A.D. 65-70)

Jude 20. But you, beloved, build yourselves up on your most holy faith; pray in the Holy Spirit.

By bringing together the two thoughts of upbuilding and praying in the Holy Spirit, Jude clearly refers to praying in tongues (see 1 Cor. 14:4, 14-15; Eph. 6:18).

It could be disturbing if we saw from heaven's vantage point how much our spiritual capacity has remained dwarfed because we have not *consistently* prayed in this way. There is little merit in receiving the gift of tongues if we rarely use it.

Hebrews (A.D. 65-70)

Heb. 2:4. God also bore witness by signs and wonders and various miracles and by gifts of the Holy Spirit distributed according to His own will.

F. F. Bruce has written:

> The testimony of the New Testament writings to the regularity with which these phenomena accompanied the preaching and receiving of the gospel in the early apostolic age is impressive in its range.... The New Testament writers ... would not have appealed to the evidence of these miraculous manifestations if there was any possibility that their readers would reply that they had never seen or heard of such things. They were matters of common knowledge and widespread Christian experience. [11]

Heb. 4:12. For the word of God is living and active, sharper than any two-edged sword, piercing to the division of soul and spirit, of joints and marrow, and discerning the thoughts and intentions of the heart.

The "word of God" here includes the written Word of God, but it is certainly not limited to it (see 1 Cor. 14:24-25; Heb. 6:5; Eph. 6:17; Col. 3:16; 1 Pet. 4:10; 2 Pet. 3:5; Rev. 1:10). As we noticed previously, it also applies to that direct word of conviction, correction or instruction delivered straight to the heart by the Holy Spirit.

Heb. 13:8. Jesus Christ is the same yesterday and today and for ever.

The Lord Jesus who "went about doing good, and healing all who were oppressed by the devil" (Acts 10:38) is the same today as He was yesterday. And He will remain so forever. This same Jesus bestowed His authority and power on His followers to do what He did (John 14:12). *They* were now His Body—the living, dynamic expression of His love and compassion toward the needy. If it had been God's plan that the world was to lose His miraculous ministry through the Spirit, the writer to the Hebrews could not have made this affirmation. It could be stated with certainty because the same Lord was continuing His life in the Church. His power and authority over "the spiritual hosts of wickedness" that constantly seek to defeat God's purpose are as great today as yesterday. His compassion is undiminished. All that He was to sick, longing, unsure, needy, sinful people, He is today. He is still the same Savior, the same Baptizer in the Spirit. Still the same Sustainer and Wonderful Counsellor. All that He has been in sending down His Spirit to work mighty acts through His Body, He is today. And the same inspiring power of Christ, sufficient then and now, will continue to be available until He returns.

1 John (A.D. 70-90)

1 John 4:1-6. Beloved, do not believe every spirit, but test the spirits to see whether they are of God; for many false prophets have gone out into the world. By this you know the Spirit of God: every spirit

which confesses that Jesus Christ has come in the flesh is of God, and every spirit which does not confess Jesus is not of God. . . . Whoever knows God listens to us. . . . By this we know the spirit of truth and the spirit of error.

In these verses, John describes how to detect false prophets and teachers. This shows that genuine revelation was continuing, for otherwise all could be eliminated. Nevertheless, supernatural manifestations in themselves do not at all prove that God is the source. John Rea comments:

> To protect a local church from false prophets, the Holy Spirit may manifest Himself through a certain member of that Body with the gift of the discerning of spirits (1 Cor. 12:10). . . . (Yet) even when the charismatic gift of discerning spirits is not manifested, Christians are responsible to examine carefully every seeming work of the Spirit. We must not quench the Spirit or despise prophetic utterances; but we are to "prove all things"—test all messages and signs—and hold fast to the genuine manifestations of the Spirit and abstain from everything which appears to be evil (1 Thess. 5:19-22; 1 Cor. 14:29). In 1 John 4:1-6 and 2 John 5-7 the Lord has given us certain tests to use in "trying" the spirits. Employing standards such as these, the church at Ephesus put certain self-styled apostles to the test and found them to be false (Rev. 2:2).[12]

Our Lord also gave us a moral test to apply when in doubt: "Beware of false prophets, who come to you in sheep's clothing but inwardly are ravenous wolves. You will know them by their fruits . . ." (Matt. 7:15-16). And John had just written, "Whoever does not do right is not of God, nor he who does not love his brother" (1 John 3:10; see 4:8; 1 Cor. 14:29).

Revelation (A.D. 90-95)

The book of the Revelation is itself a whole series of prophecies, many of which are predictive.

Rev. 2 and 3. When John wrote in turn to the seven churches, he gave them each a detailed prophecy, and because their purpose was not only local and momentary in application, they were incorporated in Scripture. In the first instance, however, they related to the current need in each local church, and which the Holy Spirit indicated required correction.

Rev. 3:20. Behold, I stand at the door and knock; if any one hears my voice and opens the door, I will come in to him and eat with him, and he with me.

The only reason we can be saved and enjoy the Lord's presence and blessing is because this verse is still gloriously applicable. Jesus has not stopped knocking, speaking or fellowshipping with our generation. He still communicates with us through the Scriptures and by direct revelation through members of His Body. This revelation will always fully accord with the written Word and glorify Him.

The church that pleases God is a listening church, alert for the sound of the Master's knock and voice.

Rev. 19:10. The testimony of Jesus is the spirit of prophecy.

This verse can either mean that the message of Jesus is the spirit, the very essence of all prophetic utterance; or that true prophetic inspiration (*pneuma*) always expresses itself in uplifting Jesus. While both are true, the latter is preferable and accords well with Jesus' words, "when the Counsellor comes, . . . even the Spirit of truth . . . he will bear witness to me" (John 15:26). *He* would reveal in breadth, depth and height the mysteries of Christ's power and love and the riches of the inheritance lavished upon us all (see Eph. 1:7-23).

By bringing together biblical material on some of the rich ministry of the Holy Spirit, we have of necessity excluded many other equally important subjects. Study on any other single doctrine such as the second coming, sanctification, baptism, the Church, ministry, election, etc., will also seem to unduly emphasize one truth. It is therefore essential that the subject of this book is seen as *one segment only of God's multi-faceted grace.*

Other than in isolated churches, the pattern of the early church's life and vitality is not being reproduced today. In this situation, we can either allow the present level of church life to mold our view of the Bible and our theology (and seek to rationalize any lack of vitality), or we can be molded by God's Word. If we take this last course, we have far greater scope to grow into the fullness of God's provision.

In seeking to find our place in God's service, our motives are extremely important. Like Naaman we may be ready to do some great thing (see 2 Kings 5:8-14)—such as being prominent in preaching, revelation or miracle where people are truly helped—but where we also receive a portion of the honor! But until our own inadequacies are dealt with, such "success" would pander to our ambition and pride, leave us content without inward change, and hinder God's work in others.

There are many more basic issues than conspicuous ministry, for God wants first to prove our love, obedience and faithfulness in the little inconspicuous things. He wants to test our desire to become like Him, so that we can more adequately represent Jesus in the world. Like Paul, our desire should be "to know him and the power of his resurrection, becoming like him in his death" (Phil. 3:8-14).

Time spent in allowing the Lord to bring our lives into divine order and being built up in Him is time well spent, and is essential if we are to lift others to full enrichment in God and to fulfill His purpose for our own lives.

NOTES

Chapter 1

1. Reprinted with permission from *First Epistle of Paul to the Corinthians*, Leon Morris, 1958, Wm. B. Eerdmans Publishing Co., p. 36.

2. See Acts 18:11. Approximate dates Sept. A.D. 50 until March A.D. 52.

3. "Regular" and "supernatural" gifts are considered in the introductory paragraphs of ch. 4. These terms represent an attempt to describe God's varied dealings with men.

4. I am indebted to Bob Mumford for this insight. See his *Christ in Session*, Bob Mumford, 1973.

5. *First Epistle to the Corinthians*, C. K. Barrett, 1968, Harper & Row, p. 295. This and other quotations reprinted by permission.

6. That "elder," "overseer" and "pastor" are equivalent is shown from Acts 20:17, 28. Paul "called to him *the elders* of the church" and said . . . " 'Take heed to yourselves and to all the flock, in which the Holy Spirit has made you guardians (overseers) *to feed* (pastor, shepherd) the church of the Lord.' " The N.T. indicates that there were several elders in each locality. Some would excel in oversight, some in teaching or in other varied ministries.

7. *Now That You've Been Baptized in the Spirit*, Donald Gee, 1972, Gospel Publishing House, p. 115. Reprinted by permission.

8. *Speaking in Tongues and Its Significance for the Church*, L.

Christenson, 1968, Bethany Fellowship, Inc., p. 114. Reprinted with permission.

Chapter 2

1. *One in the Spirit*, D.C.K. Watson, 1974, Fleming H. Revell Co. Reprinted with permission.

2. Reprinted with permission from *Gifts and Graces*, A. Bittlinger, 1973, Wm. B. Eerdmans Publishing Co., p. 87f.

3. Op. cit. 305.

4. *Annie Johnson Flint's Best-Loved Poems*, Marshall,. Morgan & Scott (undated), p. 24. Reprinted with permission.

5. Op. cit. 93. Used by permission.

6. See C. K. Barrett, op. cit. 311.

Chapter 3

1. For *pneuma* as the source of inspiration and enablement, and virtually synonymous with such divine stimulus, see also 1 Cor. 14:32; Matt. 22:43; Luke 2:27; Acts 6:10; Eph. 1:17; 5:18; 1 Thess. 5:19; 2 Thess. 2:2; 1 John 4:1-2; Rev. 22:6. Cf. Neh. 9:20, 30; Job 32:8; Isa. 11:2; Joel 2:28-29.

2. Op. cit. 320.

3. Op. cit. 319.

4. *Epistle to the Romans*, C. K. Barrett, 1958, Harper & Row, p. 39. Used by permission.

5. From *New Testament Words*, by William Barclay, © SCM Press Ltd., 1964. Index © The Westminster Press, 1974, p. 154. Used by permission.

6. This presupposes A.D. 33 as the date of Paul's conversion, and A.D. 54/55 for the writing of 1 Cor. These dates are widely accepted by scholars.

7. Op. cit. 323.

8. Nine scriptural criteria for judging prophecy are listed in Bob Mumford's practical book, *Take Another Look at Guidance* (Logos International, 1971), pp. 119-125.

9. Ibid. 121. Used by permission.

10. Op. cit. 119f. Used by permission.

Chapter 4

1. The trinitarian formula of Matt. 28:19, where baptism is to be "into the name of the Father and of the Son and of the Holy Spirit," is "appropriate for 'disciples of all the nations' (i.e., Gentiles), turning from paganism to serve the living God, whereas Jews and Samaritans, who already acknowledged the one true God, were required only to confess Jesus as Lord and Messiah." (Reprinted with permission from *Book of the Acts*, F. F. Bruce, 1954, Wm. B. Eerdmans Publishing Co., p. 181.)

2. Reprinted with permission from *Acts of the Apostles* (Greek Text), F. F. Bruce, 1953, Wm. B. Eerdmans Publishing Co., p. 187

3. The same basic Greek clause (*en logō*) is found in another charismatic context in 1 Cor. 1:5, where the noun is rendered "speech" (see 1 Cor. 2:4, etc.).

4. Reprinted with permission from *New Bible Commentary Revised*, 1970, Wm. B. Eerdmans Publishing Co., p. 983.

The same Western text is behind the RSV footnote on 8:37, where again it confirms N.T. evidence as to the nature of early Christian baptism. Both are best regarded as additions by an early commentator rather than scripture.

5. *Book of the Acts*, op. cit. 230. Used by permission.

6. See *Book of the Acts*, F. F. Bruce, op. cit. 385.

7. Grammatically, both the RSV and KJV renderings of Acts 19:2 and Eph. 1:13 are fully justified, for the aorist participle (*pisteusantes*, believing) can refer either to antecedent or coincident action—and be translated "after believing" or "when believing" respectively. "Antecedent action . . . is indeed the most common use of the aorist participle . . . (Yet) simultaneous action . . . is common also" (A. T. Robertson, *Grammar of the Greek N.T.*, 1914, p. 860). Examples of antecedent action are Matt. 4:2; John 5:13; Heb. 1:3; Mark 9:26. Examples of coincident action are Matt. 27:4; Eph. 1:20; Heb. 7:27.

Though some consider it is *doctrinally* important to understand the aorist participle as referring to coincident action in Acts 19:2 and Eph. 1:13 (and also Acts 11:17), this can only be regarded as their own theological preference. It is not a *grammatical* requirement.

The variety of meaning Paul introduced by choosing the aorist participle can best be retained by translating the former verse, "Have you received the Holy Spirit either when or after you believed?" Here and in Eph. 1:13 ("You . . . after or when you believed in him, were sealed . . . ") Paul could easily have referred to the time element in a way that would allow only one meaning. That he did not do so confirms that the precise moment of receiving the Spirit could vary. His aim was to see that the reception definitely took place, and if it had not, to rectify the situation immediately.

The Samaritans and the 12 Ephesian disciples did in fact receive the Spirit and were sealed *after* they believed, whereas this evidently happened to Cornelius and his friends *at the same time* as they believed. But either subsequently or simultaneously they received the Spirit and were sealed.

Chapter 5

1. Philip Hughes quotes Calvin, Allo and Swete in approval, and writes: "The great majority of editors and commentators are agreed in understanding the Apostle to be referring to God the Holy Spirit here, while at the same time acknowledging that the Holy Spirit cannot be separated from the gifts and graces He imparts." (Reprinted with permission from *Paul's Second Epistle to the Corinthians*, P. E. Hughes, 1962, Wm. B. Eerdmans Publishing Co., p. 228.)

2. Reprinted with permission from *Second Epistle of Paul to the Corinthians*, R.V.G. Tasker, 1958, Tyndale Press (London), and Wm. B. Eerdmans Publishing Co., p. 174f.

3. Op. cit. 443. Used by permission.

4. *Baptism in the Holy Spirit,* James D. G. Dunn, 1970, Alec. Allenson, p. 149. Reprinted with permission.

James Dunn illustrates convincingly from scripture the vivid nature of the Spirit's coming. I am unconvinced by some of his exegesis and conclusions on other points, but his book well repays careful study and leaves the reader with many helpful insights.

5. Two Greek words significant for our present purpose are used within a charismatic context in 1 Cor. (1) *pneumatikē* (spiritual, 1:3) which compares with *pneumatikōn* (spirituals, spiritual gifts)

in 1 Cor. 12:1; and (2) the noun *ploutos* (riches, copiousness, 1:7) which compares with the verb *ploutizō* (to enrich) in 1 Cor. 1:5.

6. See note 7 in ch. 4 of this book.

7. See J.D.G. Dunn, op. cit. 133. J. K. Parratt (to whom Dunn refers) writes regarding the sealing and the earnest (*arrabōn*) of the Spirit:

> *The promise* of the Spirit referred primarily to the effusion of the Spirit at Pentecost, accompanied by the charismatic gift of glossolalia .... It is possible that the *earnest* also has charismatic associations. As many commentators point out, the word *first-fruit* (*aparchē*) is used in Rom. 8:23 in the same sense as *earnest* is in the Ephesian and Corinthian epistles. According to Sanday and Headlam it is likely that this word implied the presence of the charismatic gifts (cf. *Romans*, 1902, p. 209), and if this is so, *earnest* may well indicate something similar. In this case the apostle's point will be that it is the possession of the charismatic gifts ... that constitutes the Christian's guarantee of future salvation.
>
> If this exegesis can be sustained it leads to interesting conclusions. The *seal, promise, earnest* and *first-fruits* of the Spirit will ...refer ... to the charismatic effusion of the Spirit upon the early Christian communities .... The *seal* therefore will be a charismatic effusion of the Spirit, connected no doubt with the whole process of Christian initiation, but not to be identified with baptism as such (J. K. Parratt, *"The Seal of the Holy Spirit and Baptism,"* Baptist *Quarterly* [London] 23, 1969, pp. 111-113).

8. The clause "in the Spirit" (*en pneumati*) in both these passages is the same as that in Matt. 22:43, which RSV renders as *inspired by the Spirit* (see Matt. 12:28; Luke 1:17). *En tō pneumati* is similarly rendered in Luke 2:27; Mark 12:36.

9. This RSV marginal reading is shared by various other translations. Textual evidence makes it the preferred reading.

10. The Epistle of James is difficult to date. If the author was James the Lord's brother, as seems most probable, the latest date would have to be A.D. 62, but it could be considerably earlier than that.

11. F. F. Bruce, *Epistle to the Hebrews*, Eerdmans, 1964, pp. 30f.

12. John Rea, *Layman's Commentary on the Holy Spirit*, Logos, 1972, p. 106f.